SAILING THE BAY

SAILING THE BAY

KIMBALL LIVINGSTON

CHRONICLE BOOKS   SAN FRANCISCO

For Joseph and Julia

Library of Congress Cataloging in Publication Data
Livingston, Kimball.
  Sailing the Bay.
  1. Sailing—California—San Francisco Bay. 2. Tidal currents—California—San
Francisco Bay. 3. San Francisco Bay (Calif.)—Description and travel. 4. San
Francisco Bay (Calif.)—Climate. I. Title.
GV776.C22S365   797.1'24'097946   81-3870
ISBN 0-87701-180-X   AACR2

Editing: Rain Blockley
Book and cover design: John Beyer
Typography: Type by Design

Chronicle Books
870 Market Street
San Francisco, California 94102

Acknowledgments

Wordell Johnson at the U.S. Army Corps of Engineers Bay
Model contributed information and good humor. T. John
Conomos and Ralph Cheng of the U.S. Geological Survey
did the same. G. G. Thornton and David Eames provided
inspiration. John Ravizza took me on my first sailboat
race. Lay the blame on them.

Photo Credits

Army Corps of Engineers: 46, 47

Diane Beeston: 2, 8, 12, 28, 34, 54, 70, 87

John E. Hutton: 14, 19, 22, 27, 31, 32, 59, 61, 65, 66, 68, 75, 76,
78, 80, 93

Hal Lauritzen: Cover

Kimball Livingston: 62

John O'Hara: Back cover

Frank Pedrick: 11, 83, 90

Portions of this book originally appeared in *Sail* magazine

BIBLIOGRAPHY

Clancy, Edward P. *The Tides: Pulse of the Earth.* Garden City, N.J.: Doubleday & Co., 1968.

Conomos, T. J., ed. *San Francisco Bay: The Urbanized Estuary.* Lawrence, Kansas: Allen Press. For the California Academy of Sciences, San Francisco, 1979.

Gilliam, Harold. *Weather of the San Francisco Bay Region.* Berkeley and Los Angeles: University of California Press, 1962.

Kotsch, William J., Rear Admiral, Ret. *Weather for the Mariner.* Annapolis: Naval Institute Press, 1977.

Neumann, Gerhard, and Pierson, Willard J. Jr. *Principles of Physical Oceanography.* Englewood Cliffs, N.J.: Prentice-Hall, Inc., 1966.

Newton, Sir Isaac. *Mathematical Principles of Natural Philosophy.* Translated by Andrew Motte. Berkeley and Los Angeles: University of California Press, 1934. Reprint. Chicago, London, Toronto, Geneva: Encyclopaedia Britannica, Inc., 1952.

U.S. Department of Commerce, National Oceanic and Atmospheric Administration. *Tidal Current Tables, 1981: Pacific Coast of North America and Asia.* Rockville, Maryland: National Ocean Survey.

U.S. Department of Commerce, National Oceanic and Atmospheric Administration. *United States Coast Pilot, Pacific Coast: California, Oregon, Washington, and Hawaii.* Rockville, Maryland: National Ocean Survey, 1980.

CONTENTS

FOREWORD

*K*IMBALL LIVINGSTON has been sailing and racing boats on San Francisco Bay for as long as I can readily remember. His introduction into the sailing scene as a writer for the San Francisco *Chronicle* brought a breath of fresh air to the weekly sailing results, and his comments are read enthusiastically by the thousands of avid sailors in the Bay Area. Kim has combined his knowledge of Bay sailing and his ability as a writer in a fascinating book which will be readable by either a beginner or an experienced sailor. Such nuances as tide rips around Alcatraz and wind shifts in the vicinity of Angel Island are described and discussed in details drawn from Kim's long experience of racing on the Bay.

Descriptions of wild rides underneath the Golden Gate Bridge, with the famed "Demon of the South Tower" looking over your shoulder, are fascinating, though the horrified beginner should not overlook a certain humorous intent. I particularly enjoyed Kim's lucid descriptions of the various ways to get into trouble on San Francisco Bay because they brought back memories of the very problems I have struggled with in my own 30 years of Bay sailing.

Without a doubt, San Francisco Bay is the most exciting place in the world to sail. The consistent velocity of the wind, the trickiness of the currents, the fickleness of the fog all combine to offer real challenges to any sailor. Kim Livingston attempts to solve these problems and to make sailing on the Bay more enjoyable for everybody by explaining why they happen and how they happen. Technical descriptions of natural phenomena are well researched and well documented in this book and make for interesting reading for students of meteorology.

Anyone who is fortunate enough to live in the Bay Area and to have enjoyed the pleasure of sailing on San Francisco Bay will relate to Kim Livingston's writing very directly. Anyone who has not had the pleasure of being directly involved on the Bay will be able to participate through Kim's book. The reader will be able to imagine somewhat what it must be like to sail on a blustery summer day in the windiest spot in the world.

I hope that readers of *Sailing the Bay* will enjoy it as much as I did and that the book can serve as a reference to enhance enjoyment of sailing for everyone fortunate enough to sail on San Francisco Bay.

Tom Blackaller

PREFACE

*H*ALFWAY BETWEEN PAIN AND PARADISE lives the sailor on San Francisco Bay. He has books to tell how to set sails, how to trim sails, how to take sails down. He has books to tell how to navigate to Bora Bora, but nothing to tell how to navigate out of the Berkeley Circle sideways, laid flat, soaked and chilled and thrilled and living in pain and living in paradise all at the same time. Halfway is what you get when you average the two. It is the common state of the San Francisco Bay sailor.

This book will not teach you how to sail. Sailing will teach you how to sail. This book will not teach you about currents. The struggle will teach you. This book will teach instead a few holds and a few escapes. It will wish you well. It will provide a few hard-won insights from one who has traveled the road from the Marina Green, looking out to that beautiful Bay and saying, Lord, transport me there.

Ebb tide meets west wind. This sloop's mainsail has been reefed.

I: THE DEVIL'S OWN GRIN

A STRONG CURRENT and opposing winds make a classic rough-water mix. The waves run more to the perpendicular, the troughs thin out, and the tops go to slapping salt in the face. Going to weather is mainly a science of minimizing the jolts, and in a racing dinghy the jolts come hard and fast. Only a war dance on the trapeze will keep two feet on the rail.

As for particulars . . . it was a day in March. The prudent and the already-broken made a sizable gathering on the beach to watch the fray. Most wore wet wetsuits. All had a clear idea what the diehards on the course were dealing with: wind, minus gusts, at thirty knots; the tide ebbing at four knots, brown with long whitecaps. Seen from the rocks at the city-front breakwater, the fleet seemed to stagger to windward one stubbed toe at a time. To the crowd it was clear who made a bad tack. They were swimming. In the background, as bare as during the Gold Rush, rose the northern escarpment of an ocean pass. The miners of the 1840s—and the merchants who greeted them—called it the Golden Gate. The ebb rushed out, and the wind rushed in.

After blowing unbroken across thousands of miles of open ocean, the westerlies of the Pacific pile headlong into the coastal mountains of California. Like a wind dyke, the hills survive; but if ever there was a hole in the dyke, it is the entrance to San Francisco Bay—which is nothing to think about while hanging onto a 505, looking for the layline between dousings, and talking privately to Saint Christopher.

Two million years ago a river ran through a mountain valley, flowing out through this westward cleft. But with the sea level rising and the continent folding and faulting, the mountain valley became an arm of the ocean where the yellow 505 of Jon Andron and Bob McNeil one March day moved to the front of the pack. They closed on the weather mark one stubbed toe at a time; rounded; and took off in a hail of spray. White water foamed, sails stuck out, and sometimes something yellow changed backgrounds—fast.

The crowd roared when they set the chute.

A big slice of San Francisco's vitality lives in the anything-goes, Wild-West manners that have never quite worn off. In Victorian Row, the purr of Mercedes engines blends with the rumble of chopped Harleys; on San Francisco Bay, sailboat racing is treated like busting broncs. Of course, learning to love this sort of thing can warp one.

Andron and McNeil nearly made it to the leeward mark. The crowd roared for the capsize.

After the turbulence of winter storms and the long calms between them comes spring and hot weather inland in California's central valley—a zone of low atmosphere pressure—where the overheated air rises in great spiraling thermals. At sea, moisture-laden northwesterlies cross a coastal current cooled by the upwelling of deep water. The water chills the wind. Fog forms. This dense, cold air sweeps the California coast—a zone of high pressure—blocked by the mountains from charging inland except at a few gaps in the hills and at that grandaddy gap of them all, the entrance to San Francisco Bay.

Many is the ocean racer heading home in, say, fifteen knots true who has chosen to carry The Big Chute right to the mouth of the Golden Gate. We are talking about a normal day. The skipper is in control, and the rugged rock walls rise like welcoming arms. Ahead, the overheated central valley is drawing in a mass of cold air, a big mass through a tiny opening. No matter how benign the appearance, the Devil of the South Tower lurks beneath the Golden Gate Bridge. The gusts are sudden and vicious, and only one thing can happen: the old bug-in-a-vacuum-cleaner routine: broaching to leeward, broaching to windward. Quite hard on the fillings. The forces simply wrench control from the helmsman—a powerful demonstration of Giovanni Venturi's physics concept, on a scale far beyond any textbook sketch of arrows hastening through a tube's narrowing width.

Straight downwind from this monster, the San Francisco city front and the Central Bay catch the brunt. While the wind will sometimes fairly howl wherever people sail, San Francisco Bay's summertime screamer only sometimes quits. Here the sailor has season-long access to the visceral stimulation of taking a One Tonner in enough wind for kicks around six or seven buoys, any of which on station may be doing three knots through the water. Downwind, a spinnaker, a blooper, and a reefed main will keep a thirty-seven-footer moving at white water pitch, surfing on the better waves, with every line on the boat tuned to E over High C.

Approaching the gybe mark, the point man will be listening to the chatter between trimmer and helmsman. His first job in gybing will be to douse the blooper, clearing the foretriangle for action. As he goes forward to gather the sail, others free the blooper sheet and halyard. The sail flies forward and down, collapsing into the point man's busy hands. At once the boat alters balance. The driver–trimmer chatter rises a note as the chute—its upward and outward thrust no longer offset by the blooper—oscillates: straining from side to side, and rolling as nothing on land rolls.

On the foredeck, the point man has his hands full of nylon that he must stash quickly. And he must settle the halyard, all the while working faster for knowing that his weight forward drives the bow down, forcing the bow into eccentric courses, lifting the rudder and robbing its bite. He is pumping adrenalin like a gusher, but he sees in slow motion. Above him the sky is a perfect fog. Tumbling fog, perfect. All is clear as fog: deck, sail, salt, fog. The blooper is secure. It is time to refocus.

And it clicks. It clicks as easy as calling, "Ready to gybe!" Hands outstretched, he walks to the bow. The bow digs into every trough. It wants to turn right, or it wants to turn left. The driver makes vigorous steering corrections; he plants one foot on the side of the cockpit and cries, "Ready! Gybe!" The spinnaker pole is tripped free from the clew of the sail. Its outboard end swings in toward the bow as the spinnaker lifts and the boat rolls and the spinnaker dips and lifts again and takes off with the masthead for the South Forty. The deck goes vertical. The point man's footing goes up in white water, and he hears a far, far away falsetto, "Damn! Damn! I've lost it!" He reaches reflexively but misses the pole, and then all the world is cold and wet.

Vienna, even at the height of Hapsburg power, was said to have a provincial air, with the scent of lush forests on the four winds. In San Francisco it is the salt on the westerly that keeps the senses alert. Bay, ocean, open hills to the north—and with them, often, the whitecapped tides—all are part of the view from the city's steep slopes. One of the rewards of studying San Francisco Bay is talking to agreeable people about boats and the rituals of their use; that is, sitting down with the neighbors to share a beer and a view. It is not hard to find people who are amenable to this sort of thing, and some of them hold strong opinions about their home waters. Take Lu Taylor, who told us early in a winning season for a boat that he called *Racy*, "Why, if it weren't for San Francisco Bay I'd get the hell out of here. I'd have my business someplace where it belongs. But I can't do that.

Sure, we sail a lot in survival conditions. It keeps you on your toes!"

There also are saner voices about. Poppy Truman, who once won the women's national sailing championship, calls Bay sailing simply "a challenge."

After all, many people live in California solely for personal safety, knowing that someday an earthquake of epic proportions will tip the rest of the country into the Atlantic with a single, massive groan. But wherever they live, there are people who *must* sail. What proliferates on San Francisco Bay as elsewhere is the simple sailing nut. How simple? is not a polite question. But a steady diet of fifteen- to twenty-five-knot winds is going to have some effect on San Francisco Bay sailors, if only in the effort to adapt.

Dave Allen is a grownup who remembers very well the kid he once was and the kids he once knew, walking to school in shirtsleeves in the cold wind and fog and summertime sailing in the same, "to see how long we could take it. Foul weather gear wasn't worth much in those days anyway." With his very successful string of ocean racers, including the fabled *Imp*, Allen has sampled the sailing all around the world, but his boats spend most of their lives berthed at the San Francisco Yacht Club. For Allen, the joy of sailing in home waters has to do with the beauty of the place, and of course the excitement of the West Bay wind funnel, but also the handy alternative of ducking into the lee of a hill to catch a sunbaked lunch. "On the Bay," Dave Allen says, "you can pick your weather." What he does not mention is having to sail through a runaway Maytag cycle to reach one's weather, or to get home. Although Allen would not trade anything for his home sailing, or for the toughened local breed, he has seen enough of the world to add that, "The Aussies and New Zealanders are also a rugged lot."

Which returns us to something basic: the second dunking is never so cold as the first, and the sailing nut sails in what he's got.

Angel Island, true to her name, is warm and toasty in the lee.

Six miles east of the Golden Gate wind funnel lies the shallow, mud-bottomed Berkeley Circle. Tides here make an (almost) simple sweep, without the complexity of current and eddy found elsewhere in the Bay, so this area is often used to minimize local knowledge advantages in major championships. With heavy air expected at the Kiel Olympics (it wasn't), the U.S. summer Olympic Trials of 1972 were held on the Bay to put hair on contenders' chests. Some have been flecked with gray ever since.

Homer could have scripted the Berkeley Circle scene: the short, white, wall-sided chop of gale over shallow water and strong men torn upon the rack of the gobbly sea. What comes back to Tom Blackaller is an image of spray-blinding white water reaches "like going into a fire hose that's shooting twenty knots." The water, that is. The wind on the final Trials day gusted to fifty, and the breakables broke. And as for two-time world champion Blackaller's late Star? "Well, I just sailed it under." He will say no more. But Blackaller is San Francisco through and through, and he hastens to remind us that the series as a whole was not so rough, "Until the last day we never saw *any* winds over twenty-five knots." Such comfort.

Fifty-knot gusts are a bad bear and a rare event even in this windy spot. But thirty knots and gusting (not so rare) still blows salt in your eye sooner than tears can wash it away. In those conditions, a race course is littered with crack, crash, and burn victims, and only the strong survive. It was like that for the 505 fleet we left staggering to windward one stubbed toe at a time. On that day in March, even the crash-boat drivers were crying for mercy as the survivors entered the final leg. At the head of the pack, Harriet Minkwitz trapezed to the finish, skimming the foam off the wavetops—most of them—and half-drowned in the rest. Minkwitz has been racing every dinghy she could get her hands on for years, and she likes this kind of sailing just fine, "as long as you're with somebody you know can swim, really well." She has the devil's own grin.

From which Harriet's driver, Hank Jotz, deduces another basic: "When the going gets weird, the weird get going."

Sic semper furiosus. When San Francisco Bay's natural ventilation system is registering at the top of its thrills-per-minute scale, sending boats to the start is like throwing Christians to the lions. But the Christians, including those who ought to know better, continue queuing up for the ride. Take the strange case of Corry and Jimmy, two fellows who after all did not retire from sailing that day they closed but good on the weather mark. They were holding good position in their dinghy fleet when it came time to tack. In the tack was a *bump*, the kind that provokes the question: Oh Heavens, Aunt Martha! What have we hit now?

But the boys trimmed right on out on the new tack, and they let their reflexes bring the boat back to speed, gathering stability enough for a look around the boat only to find themselves richer by one shark, just like that. It was a modest shark, of a species of no great reputation, and mortified at its error, but a shark nonetheless—about four feet worth of sand shark wedged right by the centerboard trunk. Jimmy sat with his feet in the straps, steering with the tiller extension. He began to ease the sails. His voice was not normal, and he was saying *"Out! Out! Get him out!"* Boats were sailing right past them. "Get him *out!*"

Corry was meanwhile hanging outside the boat on the trapeze wire and eyeballing the shark. The shark's tail was twitching one Sunday punch at a time. One shark eye was staring right back at him, and Corry looked over and said, "*You* get him out." A credit to the crew's union, that boy.

In the background, as bare as during the Gold Rush, rose the northern escarpment of the Golden Gate.

"Dammit, Corry, it's your boat!"

The air was crystal clear.

"Are you kidding? That's a *shark*!"

Two million years ago a river ran through a mountain valley, flowing out through this westward cleft. The waters rushed out, and the winds rushed in . . .

Then all the photographers in San Francisco chipped in, and they built a bridge. . . .

II: UNDERWAY ON THE BAY

*F*OUR HUNDRED TWENTY square miles on the surface, two trillion gallons in the volume. Give or take a bunch, that is the San Francisco Bay. The Bay is never quiet. The moon draws her tides. Sea waters press in as the rivers press out. Strong currents oppose, bypass, or marry. The Golden Gate, the only sea-level breach in the coastal range of mountains, admits the Pacific. It admits too the weather of the Pacific at an unpacific rate. Sea meets continent. Sea weather meets land weather, and the San Francisco Bay becomes the front line. It is a fine place to sail a boat, and a demanding one.

A hundred years ago, all San Franciscans were in tune with the ways of sail. Many had sailed to California, or they took weekend trips under sail to outlying towns. A good yacht race—or better yet, a Master Mariners race for working craft—was guaranteed to cut business in the saloons and bring forth fat pools among the wagerers on Telegraph Hill. Today the city and its environs have many inhabitants who are strangers to sail, yet the waters around us shape our thoughts. Watch on a sharp morning the commuters from Marin, riding south on Golden Gate Transit. Watch them setting aside their *Chronicles* for whatever time it takes the bus to span the Golden Gate. They sit feet crossed at the ankles, staring mutely out to sea. "There is magic in it," wrote Herman Melville. "Let the most absent-minded of men be plunged in his deepest reveries—stand that man on his legs, set his feet a-going, and he will infallibly lead you to water."

With a little forethought, San Francisco Bay can be sailed the easy way, in the warm hours from the warm anchorages. But there are those who cannot resist the call of the wild. In the summertime, the wind slot is right there for those who want it, and it is usually busy. For anyone already expert in the ways of boats, the Bay merely adds a few elements of its own: not the strongest currents in the world, but challenging; not the strongest winds in the world, but challenging, too. For those brand new to boats and still stumped between porthole and starboard, the Bay will enforce a higher level of learning than an inland lake where the water is probably warm and any wind, sans storm, is mild. The average surface temperature at the Golden Gate is 56 degrees—not a forgiving environment at the natural level. And through the Golden Gate course rivers of salt and sweet waters at rates that sometimes exceed five million cubic feet per second—many times the volume of the lower Mississippi River.

For all the conviction charging the air, no one really knows whether it was Sir Francis Drake's *Golden Hinde* in 1579 or Juan Manuel de Ayala's *San Carlos* in 1775 that first crossed the threshold of the Golden Gate. We know for certain of Ayala's passage. He came looking for the broad bay that his Spanish confederates, after long years of missing the straits from seaward, had discovered at last by land six years before, purely by accident. Captain Gaspar de Portola's party had suffered the embarrassment of mule-training right past Monterey. Their backtracking would be arduous, but the discovery was major. As Portola gazed upon his find, he surmised that this expanse must somehow connect with the protected waters around Point Reyes, where Spanish ships customarily stopped for supplies and refurbishing.

Ayala when he came would learn otherwise, but only after making a hard trip of it through the strait. The countercurrent, ebbing powerfully against the westerly, set up a forbidding, whitecapped welcome to strange waters. It was dark when the *San Carlos* at last cleared the narrows and turned north to the closest lee shore. Anchor watch was a happy duty by comparison. Morning found the *San Carlos* swinging to the hook opposite a clump of willows—a *sauzalito*. Later the ship set out to explore the Bay, stopping in what we now call Ayala Cove and giving a name to the Isla de Nuestra Señora de los Angeles (Angel Island). Many a Sunday cruise has followed Ayala's path. The *San Carlos* nosed into much of the Bay, sampling the South Bay and sailing as far east as the river beyond Carquinez Strait. That was far enough to convince the captain that he was seeing not an arm of Tomales Bay, but a grand refuge from the Pacific Ocean, a harbor of great strategic significance.

Man has since made the Bay a safer place by installing buoys, lighthouses, and foghorns. But man has also complicated the Bay with his presence. On a busy day, the water is thick with pleasure boats. Fishermen ply their trade, and the shipping lanes are active with the passage of tankers and freighters, barges under tow, naval aircraft carriers, and tugs running to and fro. It is not the same Bay it once was. Man's influence has been sudden, unlike the hand of nature, though nature has been more thorough.

Hardly could Ayala have imagined the very different landscape that once lay here, long before his time, when the ocean lapped at beaches far to the west. The Farallon Islands heard the crash of surf. The shores of this high valley were populated by camel, bison, and ground sloth species long since extinct. There was no Bay to be discovered then, but three times before there had been. In the slow turning of geologic time, thrice the ocean had invaded, backing up the rivers, changing the land. And three times the ocean had retreated. These were the ice ages, going and coming. Whenever the planet chilled and the ice pack grew, the waters shrank. When the planet warmed, the waters would flow again. The ocean would grow, and the Bay would be reborn. The last ice age ended some fifteen thousand years ago; and with the rising of the waters, inch by inch, began the fourth installment of San Francisco Bay: the one Ayala discovered, the one we sail. How long ago the first tribes settled here we do not know. The ancestors of the Miwok and Costanoan tribes passed the generations hunting and gathering. Theirs were among the simplest of the continent's native cultures when the explorers came. Their ancestors' homesites—if they existed ten to fifteen thousand years ago—would have been near the stream beds, long since flooded and scoured clean by the tides. We do not know whether it was whimsy, or artful guesswork, or memories handed down through the generations, that lay behind the native tales recorded in 1818 by Mariano Payeras of oak groves where now lies the port of San Francisco, and of a river that passed at the foot of the hills.

For a mere forty-six years after Ayala, the royal Spanish flag took the sun in this place. The Spanish repaired ships, traded illegally with Russian fur hunters, and built a mission to instill guilt in the heathen. They built also a few houses and perfunctory forts, but they left the natural order untouched. The Miwok paddling his high-ended tule raft still recognized his home. The brief day of Mexican rule saw even less change.

Quite a contrast, that, with the westward expansion of the United States. Within a decade after Fremont's conspirators had raised the flag of the Bear, there sprang up a city with rich banks at the intersections, tall ships in the harbor, and ferries scurrying to outlying settlements. The Farallon Islands were rapidly pillaged of murre eggs. Saloons and churches boomed. And one hundred years after the Bear

Flag's quick metamorphosis into the State of California, 37 percent of the Bay had disappeared to shoaling, diking, and landfill. Hydraulic mining in the Sierra stirred great volumes of mud that rode the streams tumbling down from the mountains. Much of this mud was deposited in Suisun and San Pablo bays, raising the bottom by several feet before geologic time could wink an eye.

It is this much-altered body of water that today is watched over by the Twelfth Coast Guard District. It is home to pleasure boats by the thousands, from kayaks to grand yachts. It is the shining jewel of a great city. Not only the forces of ocean and continent meet here, but the forces of wilderness and urbanization as well. The Pacific is wilderness, and the Bay draws a wild salt scent to the empty wards of Alcatraz, to the deer and raccoon of Angel Island, to the bicycle messengers of Montgomery Street. However urban the shoreline, however trafficked the shipping lanes, just a few meters of water between shoreline and transom will clear the city dweller of city cares. There is no way, overland, to get so far away so fast as motoring, sailing, rowing, drifting, or dreaming on San Francisco Bay.

Getting Started

When the boat bug bites, it bites deep. The obvious reaction, for anyone in the chips, is to rush out and buy a boat. But that may be moving too fast. Sausalito once hosted a bright yellow sloop, about twenty-six feet long, whose new owner could talk about nothing else. It was his first boat. He spent day after animated day aboard, scrubbing, fingering the gear, or talking to his neighbors in the harbor. Sometimes he relaxed in the parking lot in his green school bus. On the side of the bus was a painting of Smokey the Bear and the legend, "Only you can prevent forest fires." "Saves hassles," he said. "The cops never look twice." At night he would fire up the bus for home, there to read about boats and sailing. The next day would find him back, puttering,

watching the fog roll over the hill, and talking. Always talking.

He had never, ever, sailed. He had even purchased the boat without so much as taking it away from the dock. And there was something in his manner, as if he had passed up the test sail because he was a bit—well—intimidated. A committee of neighbors was therefore formed to get the new skipper on the road; and after dark ages of delay, a date was set. The morning came mild and clear. The Army Corps of Engineers' debris-picker *Coyote* passed, outbound in the channel, while the auxiliary was warmed up and lines were cast off. For two of the three people aboard, it was just another day out, an opportunity to touch yet another boat and to share their sailing fervor with a new recruit.

In the lee of Sausalito's Banana Belt, they hoisted the mainsail and a working jib. They ghosted slowly in a faint easterly, an eddy from the westerly breeze coming off the hill. It should have been idyllic. The first haywire sign came when one crewman bent down to shut off the motor and the owner shouted a high, plaintive, "NO!" Brows furrowed slightly, but after some cajoling and reassurance, the iron wind was duly put to sleep. The moment was given over to the peaceful lapping of water past the hull. They sailed slowly past the magnificent schooner *Wander Bird*, then barely begun on her long road to a pristine, Bristol-fashion restoration. As they passed the restaurants, early brunchers looked on with approval. Through it all, the boat's new owner sat wide-eyed, intense.

The yellow sloop soon passed out of the wind eddy. The sails went slack, then filled with the westerly, and the boat gained speed. Off the bow, far across the Bay, the steel towers of commerce were backlighted and blue in the morning. Close off the bow lay Sausalito's Hurricane Gulch. (A nineteenth-century real estate developer once tried to hang the handle of Shelter Cove on this neighborhood, which catches the wind blocked by a high ridge from downtown Sausalito. No way, Jose.)

The day's seabreeze was young, and there were no big blasts. Two-penny puffs rippled across the water. And even though there was forewarning—to ease the sails for the puffs—there was wind enough to bring the boat suddenly to fifteen degrees of heel.

"Start the motor!" said the owner, staccato.

"What?" said the crew. "What?"

"Start the motor! Take the sails down! I want to go in. *Now!*"

Silence.

"You want to what?"

The next day a For Sale sign hung on the mast. Grass soon grew around the waterline, and Smokey the Bear disappeared from the parking lot. It is a sad story. A sawbuck's worth of sailing lessons would have saved this fellow a heap of time and trouble, and probably some money.

For those who have never been there, the world of boats is confusing and so thick with information that it seems downright contradictory. Sometimes it actually is; more often it is merely perverse. Newcomers have the joys of learning, to wit: a northerly wind blows *from* the north; a northerly current sets *toward* the north. One's right hand may point east, west, north, or south, but the starboard (right) side of a boat is always and only starboard. Boats are a wonderful world to inhabit, and most of that world's stories have no ending. They continue happily. For most, when the boat bug bites, it chews in and itches forever: one does not just want a boat, one *needs* a boat. Yet it is difficult for neophytes to know just what they need in a boat until they have used a few. It is one thing to see a boat and fall in love; marriage via the pink slip is a different matter. And whether you are buying or just trying to learn, the easiest part is to find folks willing to regale you with nautical expertise. The hard part is to separate a blowhard from the genuine article.

For the beginner, sailing lessons are a capital investment. Unlearned sailors in our difficult waters are dangerous to themselves and others. They suffer many embarrassments and probably have little fun. In the best of all worlds, friends will take them along, sometimes on big boats, sometimes on small. In the real world, though, newcomers may find themselves looking for a handy sailing school. These schools are easy to find in just about any corner of the Bay; an abundance of books exists to explain sailing to beginners, intermediates, and the advanced. Book learning and on-the-water experience work together well, each building upon the other. Whether a sailor's instruction comes from friends or from professionals, one fact should impress: good boat handling is done with quiet ease. Hollering is not a good sign. If your teacher is a screamer, keep looking.

Clubs, schools, and civic organizations provide beginning and advanced instruction in sailing. Universities in the Bay Area also turn out first-rate sailors. For those new to boats, valuable public instruction is offered by the U.S. Coast Guard Auxiliary and the U.S. Power Squadrons. Directed toward the new boat-owner, their basic boating courses have only a small materials fee. Terminology, rules of the road, knot-tying, and safety tips are only a few of the topics, and there are other benefits. In class, friendships can be struck with others who are launching a new hobby (and who may have interesting boats). Successful completion of the basic course may lower the cost of insurance or open the door to advanced studies in navigation and seamanship.

The Coast Guard Auxiliary is administered by the Coast Guard, but its members are nonmilitary. Besides offering free classes, Auxiliary members in Northern California participate in the Courtesy Motorboat Examinations program and often aid at marine events. The Power Squadron is fraternal, with some eighty thousand members nationwide. When it was first formed in 1914, there was a special need for education in the ways of motorboats, but the Power Squadron has long since included sail in its instructional program.

For those short on the means to buy a boat—and who find cruising invitations hard to come by—another possibility is

An El Toro:
childhood trainer,
lifetime playground.

19

to join a racing crew. This is not for everyone; nevertheless, once the basic skills are mastered, any healthy and loyal enthusiast can find a boat to crew. It may take time. It may take hanging around the docks, putting notices on bulletin boards (not very effective), and suffering some rejections. It may even take sailing with some real turkeys for the sake of experience. But it is possible, in a few years' time, to become good enough at this to be sailing your pants off year round, or to find yourself cringing at the sound of another Friday night phone call because you've already told three skippers, "Sorry, I'm committed."

Crewing races is a gimmick that works as well for women as men. Some jobs on a fifty-footer depend on bullish strength—more than most people have—but the most valuable commodities on the average boat are stamina and skill or, in a beginner, a good attitude. So many women are already racing so successfully on the Bay that it should not be too difficult for another to find an opening. There also are a number of all-women crews, a good way to go particularly for those family women who have trouble with trial-and-error learning (which is essential) when the family is around.

The problem with crewing, for anyone who becomes serious about competition, is that most of the openings are on boats over twenty-five feet. Sooner or later will come an overwhelming urge to steer and call the shots, and the best way to develop these skills is not in big boats, but in dinghies.

One rule to understand, gender aside, is that the atmosphere on a racing boat is by nature competitive. Whenever strangers sail a race together, part of that competitive drive goes into establishing the pecking order. Sailors go through this all over again whenever they change boats. Among experts, it becomes an exercise in personality management. For beginners, it is more a matter of figuring out who to take direction from, then concentrating on the job at hand. The less glamorous jobs on a thirty-six-footer—such as tending the foreguy on a spinnaker run—are no less meaningful to success than tending the spinnaker sheet itself. And any job ill-performed can cause injuries, break expensive gear, or blow a lead.

The Foreguy

The spinnaker sheet needs intelligent tending all the time. The foreguy is merely a downhaul helping control the spinnaker pole. It is adjusted only when the position of the spinnaker pole is changed. The foreguy "follows" the pole. Tending it is a following job, so there is a tendency to go dreamy in the beauty of the boats and the way water picks up the colors of sails and the colors shimmer and heave until you're brought around with a loud, "Foreguy! For Chrissake! Would you please ease the foreguy?"

There is no single answer to the question of what kind of boat is right for San Francisco Bay. If a tiny one suits your needs—a centerboard dinghy perhaps—you will be blessed with fewer storage problems than those who go sailing in bigger boats—boats with lids—that stay in the water, somewhere, nearly all the time. Increasing numbers have meant increasing expense and difficulty in berthing. With a centerboarder, you will be learning the basics in a basic boat. That is an excellent idea. And you will have no less a yacht.

The larger the boat, the easier it is for the beginner to find himself overhorsed—and the more care is needed in the choice. Any used boat over twenty-five feet or so should be checked by a qualified surveyor. Sailors are nothing if not opinionated; and because they are mere flesh and blood, and divided along certain lines like the rest of humanity, some of them have informed opinions while others bear passionate convictions. Learning to tell which is which takes being around long enough to develop some opinions of your own—or convictions, if you prefer. Yachts are not purchased for rational reasons, so who can call the rights and wrongs? A forty-year-old, gaff-rigged schooner will not go to weather in the Golden Gate wind funnel with a modern, fiberglass sloop of the same length. It will not have as much room below, and it will eat up much, much more time and money in maintenance. But the wooden boat has an aura, and maybe a soul, that cannot be created on the prolific production lines of Costa Mesa.

Boats with accommodations below are loosely classified as cruisers or cruiser-racers, though cruiser-racer is a term rarely heard unless a point is being made. Many who want a forty-footer start out instead with a twenty-five-footer, then move up when confidence, skill, and the pocketbook say, "Go."

Whatever the size range, consider your athletic skill and personality. There are those who belong in a hotrod boat, with big thrills potential and correspondingly strong demands on those who handle it in strong winds. Others belong in a boat that takes care of itself: a heavier boat, with a fuller underbody, that imparts a feeling of stability and security—a boat that will sail itself in a straight line without fiddling, a nonathlete's boat. Either type can be pleasurably cruised or pleasurably raced, as the case may be. The full displacement boat, however, will provide a comfortable platform for watching the hotdogs do the "Alcatraz roll." It will also provide a comfortable platform for watching them blast right by. There are no right or wrong types of boats, only right or wrong reasons for buying them.

When water casts its spell, one of the high-risk bewitchments is the urge to build a boat and sail around the world. There have been some famous and inspiring successes in this group. There have also been cases of partly-finished hulls showing up in the San Francisco classifieds at "please, please buy me" prices. For those already skilled in building or ocean cruising, we can drop the word risk; but it is amazing how many people have spent two, three, or even five years in a backyard in Pacifica or Vallejo or San Jose working on a boat that was not right in the first place, does not look good, and will not sell for much. And it is amazing how many people will build a boat to cross oceans without first learning to sail.

Stories surface from time to time about the person who went to sea knowing nothing but learned underway, saw the world, and loved it. The failures receive less advertising. On the West Coast, those who make it all the way to a finished boat tend to rally in San Diego and never leave. San Diego is the last continental American port before jumping off to Never Never Land, and the eastern cove of San Diego's Shelter Island is rarely without a few examples of dreams broken upon the discovery that the Pacific is not the most convenient place for sunbathing and sybaritic joy. To be sure, there

The Murray Peterson schooner Coaster, *originally the designer's own, competing in a Master Mariners Regatta.*

are days when sun, sea, sky, and heart glow with one smile. The dolphins come to call, yakking and blowing and riding the foam of the bow wave. The Pacific in its smiling mood is close to paradise. At night the moon is so bright, white sails glow, richly silvered as Japanese silk. But the sea, first of all, is wilderness. The sea has power and beauty, good tempers and bad, but no mind. Some take to that, some do not. According to the individual, wilderness is either liberating or appalling. If blue water voyaging is the object, there is no middle attitude.

For all the lure of distant lands and sparkling waters, most boats live their lives close to home. Few totally unsuitable boats reach the new-boat market on San Francisco Bay. Some of the boats built in Southern California are lightly rigged for the light winds there; their stock gear might blow up immediately in a stiff Bay westerly. Where that is the case, most Northern California dealers have long since learned to avoid embarrassments by doing their own rigging. Many modern boats are designed, built, and used as weekenders rather than as serious sea boats. They do a little coastwise port-hopping at most. Their owners do not need, and would not care to pay for, construction appropriate to a world cruiser. This is a reasonable concept, and one could hardly argue with the famous designer whose article in an eastern magazine explained that his latest model for a certain major manufacturer was conceived for just that weekending market, with the assumption the hulls would never have to withstand extreme conditions. It seemed odd, however, that the same issue carried a full-color advertisement of that boat, touting it as a yacht for the seven seas.

Natural antipathy of some kind is alleged between "rag men" and "stinkpotters"—abhorrent terms both, and best forgotten. It is a blessing to love all boats great and small. How could anyone use the word stinkpotter after sampling the view from a grand yacht, twenty feet above the wave, with Camembert and Beaujolais? If I am planing along on a tiny Laser, I savor the thrills. With the wind high and the water near, it is difficult to identify with a sailing cousin charging to weather on some big lead mine (so called for the lead ballast in the keel). But if I am the one on a big, forceful keel yacht, with bunks for the taking and an ice chest full of Calistoga, those little mosquitos look mighty skittish and cold. When some shrieking motorboat flies by, exploding the peace and quiet, I wrinkle my nose; but just put me in the driver's seat and watch me go. Those sailboats seem so *slow*. Yet, what could compare with the gentle, thorough workout of a morning row in an up-to-the-minute, hundred-year-old Whitehall in communion with the cormorants and seals? This much I know: the best kind of yachting is whatever I am doing when the question is posed.

Making It Tick

If any single trend runs through yachting's modern history, it is what the auto industry has learned to call downsizing. It once was the custom for the large craft produced for the elevated gentlemen of Britain's Royal Yacht Squadron to make at least a bow toward the improvement of naval architecture. These brigantine yachts engaged in maneuvers with the Royal Navy (try a tax dodge like that today); Lord Belfast's *Waterwitch* bested them so badly in the 1830's that public opinion soon forced the Admiralty to buy her. The schooner yacht that won the 100 Guineas Cup from the Royal Yacht Squadron in 1851—the America's Cup—was no wee chick: the *America* was 101 feet long. In 1893 the America's Cup was defended by *Vigilant*, 124 feet long. But grand yachting was cresting then. In 1980 the America's Cup was defended by the *Freedom*, length 64 feet. And as the eighties dawned, the International Yacht Racing Union was busily incorporating Windsurfers as an international class and finding a berth in the Olympics for boardsailing.

It follows that sailing is not the exclusive sport it once was, when all boats were custom-built of wood. Long-distance cruising and racing have become commonplace rather than exceptional; and local waters, including San Francisco Bay, now attract crowds. Along with the boom in the boating population has come a boom in sailing associations and yacht clubs. No one needs a club, of course, to enjoy a boat. The waters are free, which is one of the best enticements for anyone looking for total escape. Others find that club membership opens even more good sides of the sailing life; and clubs, for the most part, are not exclusive.

The Bay Area features clubs to fit every budget and taste. Some lean toward families who like to cruise, some toward racing dinghies, and some toward racing big boats. Still others are populated by the owners of motorboats with a yen this way or that (the West Coast Outboard Association, for example, has many Bay Area members even though most of its hydroplane and runabout competitions are held in inland lakes). The smaller the club, the more likely it is to specialize; the larger, the more likely it is to have members of all persuasions.

Yacht club membership is required to enter all but a very few competitive events. This contributes a form of accountability, as well as a medium of exchange. Clubs with a sailboat-racing membership become constituents in turn of the Yacht Racing Association, Small Yacht Racing Association, Small Boat Racing Association, Predicted Log Racing Association, and so on. These organizations plan the season schedule, and the clubs then take turns sponsoring the races. Many budget-minded groups provide a reasonable way for the newcomer to get started and to get around. "Paper clubs" exist in large part to provide entrée to regattas at minimum cost. That cost—initiation fees and a year's dues—can be less than the going rate for topsiders.

A listing of clubs—complete with rosters of officers and member yachts—can be found in the *Yachting Year Book*, a valuable guide published by the Pacific Inter-Club Yacht Association. The PICYA has sixty-five member clubs, and its yearbook contains historical data, the rosters of many one-design classes, and information about the yacht, small-yacht, and small-boat racing associations that make the sport tick.

Organized in 1896, the PICYA also sponsors Opening Day, an enduring tradition on both the Bay and Delta. Since springtime these days leaves nothing much to open on Opening Day, we have instead a cheerful anomaly—a reminder of eastern traditions that took hold when the sport was young, then were subverted to our own Wild West purposes. In the early days of San Francisco yachting, boats were laid up for the winter, eastern style, and the games resumed in the spring. A number of harbors, including the Belvedere Lagoon, were favorite wintering holes. The entrance to that lagoon was filled in 1926; but until then, a drawbridge linked a narrow, sandy strip of Tiburon to the Belvedere hill. That bridge could be raised at any time, for a fee, but there also was a time each spring when it would open for the freshly varnished fleet to pass in force to the Bay. There they would join boats from South San Francisco and the East Bay, sail west into the strait, and then—in the afternoon—parade the city front with all flags flying.

The several-score yachts that participated each year in Opening Day had skippers who, for the most part, were not strangers to each other. If they did not meet on the water, they met in town—after all, they owned it. Yachting has since gone from a closely held preserve to a public and popular pastime. Not just the fiberglass production line but the rise of deficit financing have brought us to a sailing population of thousands and a fiesta time—Opening Day—wedged into a busy spring calendar. Many of the yachts that come out have sailed right through the winter, and some are already a month deep in their annual ocean-racing series. Yet the racers and the cruisers, the trawlers and canoes *do* turn out for Opening Day. It is the one day of the year that is meant for everyone.

Festivities kick off in Raccoon Strait with a Blessing of the Fleet, sponsored by Corinthian Yacht Club. From there, a long parade tours the city front of San Francisco. There are parties and bands and everybody and his great uncle's third cousin out to celebrate. Also present are the sailing equivalents of the Christmas-and-Easter churchgoer: people who will not use their boats again until Labor Day. Given the levels of crowding and inebriation one may witness on Opening Day, and the many infrequent sailors out and about, the situation is not entirely undangerous. Which lends a certain poignance to the Blessing of the Fleet.

Opening Day is also a time for relaxing in the quiet coves of Marin, which are not so quiet on Opening Day. Some boats skip the parades and arrive early. In the warm, protected lees of Angel Island and Tiburon, hundreds of boats drop anchor, haul out the wine and cheese, and make a day of it right there.

Given the crowds and the scads of inexperienced hands buzzing around in boats, it is an amazement there are no line-ups of Opening Day ambulance cases. Perhaps by way of compensation, there are always certain sights to justify a wince: anchors and anchor rodes become fouled, sails improperly hoisted fall down, there are jibs with scallops, and hordes of green yachties trundle about with fenders dangling over their sides—a huge faux pas. These offending fenders are derided as "Marina del Rey racing stripes" by sailors all over California (except those in Marina del Rey, naturally). Under way, fenders over the side become unsightly and unseamanlike. Of course, anyone at one time or another can forget to pull in the fenders after leaving the dock; the one mistake made only by new kids on the block is to sail with a scalloped jib. When a headsail is properly hoisted, its leading edge (the *luff*) is taut. When the jib halyard is not given enough tension, the sail will bag and sag into scallops. It is unattractive, inefficient, bad for the sail, and all too common among those who rush out onto the Bay without proper schooling. Opening Day, for all the good times, has more than its share of such sights. They can only lead one to muse, "I hope they learn. I hope they learn. It is going to be a long season."

So Sail Away

What the California coast lacks in the way of easy cruising grounds, the San Francisco Bay and Delta make up. In the center arena, the West and Central bays probably see more traffic than anything short of the Bay Bridge approach ramp. Visitors are awed by the beauty. Natives see, yet do not lose their wonder. The crazy steeples and spires and gingerbread of the city that sometimes knows how; the unspoiled Marin headlands rising in tiers to the profile of the Miwoks' Sleeping Princess, Tamalpais; the rush of the seabreeze—the sailor is immune to feeling trapped in the city.

A magazine editor from New York once took a boat ride on the Bay with a local newspaperman. "It's gorgeous," said the editor. "I mean, it's alive and the colors are strong, and it's nature, and the nature is big. But then, you're too much accustomed to it. We have to travel *so* far to taste something like this, but you probably don't even notice, since you live here."

"Wrong," said his companion. "Every morning I wake up and I look out here. I walk to the window, and I just stand there and stare."

Northern California waters merit exploring well into the shallows of the South Bay, into the small-boat racing alleys of Palo Alto and the speedboat stretches of Redwood City. Along the eastern reach, a bustling channel leads past the railway yards, the shipping docks, the U.S. Navy's jet strip, and the spoils of industry to Oakland Harbor and Alameda. In the Oakland Estuary rests, somewhere, every manner of craft from the giants of international commerce to the most mundane and exotic of yachts. The neighborhoods are also thick with people who know how to handle and service such machinery—and with the watering holes where they meet. Munchtime focus of the East Bay's thriving yachting industry is the Rusty Pelican, with its reputation as the Citizen's Yacht Club of Alameda. Overhead, the beamed ceiling carries appropriate quotations—the likes of Arthur Dettner

Jr.'s "I don't mind if you write your name in the water, but you don't have to go back to read it," or R. C. Keefe's "Wake me when the weather moderates."

Much more countrified, though far from wilderness, are the small creeks and rivers that flow into San Pablo Bay via Petaluma, Sonoma, and Napa. There is a charm to be found in these northern towns, an escape from the fast pace and cool temperatures that front the Golden Gate. And should these tire, the Delta country adds another thousand miles of navigable waterways through rivers and sloughs and marshland, waterways carrying their traffic high above the low-lying, diked farmlands. Marinas and restaurants lurk around the bend for those who want them. For the quiet-minded there is always an isolated tule bank whose most oppressive racket comes from the humming of a bee or the whistling of a meadowlark across a plowed field. The smokestack of a freighter may pass in the distance, bound upriver to Sacramento or Stockton by its own route. The Delta pace is as slow as one might wish, the people are friendly, and the wind is warm.

An upriver cruise can be the perfect escape from the paradise of the Bay. These waters that front the Golden Gate have everything a sailor could want except a tropical climate and coconuts for the picking. The Bay also has enough boats, one would think, to raise the level of the water: there are days when regatta crosses regatta, weaving the warp and woof of a fleeting fabric in a dodge'em–scare'em game not recommended for the faint of heart. Fishing cadres stake out their territories, ferries snort around, and one may encounter anything from a seventy-mile-per-hour Scarab to a mid-bay swimmer wearing nothing but a red cap, a pearl necklace, and a big, oblivious smile.

The Bay is open range, almost, but there are rules written and unwritten. Among the unwritten rules, good manners suggest that cruising boats give way to racers. This is common practice, the theory being that the cruiser is in no hurry while the racer is probably wound up tight and fighting for every inch. Always the preferred method is to pass the racing boat to leeward so as never to come between the racer and the wind: a sailing boat casts a windshadow several times the height of its mast.

The cruiser can easily cope with one racing boat at a time. In practice, however, there are days when no matter where the cruising yacht goes, no matter which way the cruiser turns, somebody is coming on yelling, "Racing! We're racing!" When confronted by a whole wall of boats, maybe even two walls from different directions, the cruiser may well be trapped. It becomes impossible to keep off everyone's wind.

Racing sailors on days like this must master a few courtesies of their own. It is not very often that an encounter with a cruising boat has cost anyone a race, much less a season's championship, and life is too short for the bad-mouthing that sometimes ensues—which is not to excuse the cruising yacht from making an intelligent effort.

Starting areas for races should always be avoided by non-contestants. Races are usually started at a "line" between a committee boat and a buoy. On the Bay, however, races are sometimes started from shore—along the San Francisco Marina breakwater, for example, where both the Golden Gate and St. Francis yacht clubs have permanent buoys established in-line with their race decks. It is possible to second-guess the direction the racing boats will take after they start: their first mark will almost always be directly upwind; downwind starts are rare.

Races are started by the stopwatch—usually on a ten-minute countdown, with a white shape signaling ten minutes to start, a blue shape signaling five minutes, and a red shape signaling the start. Where guns or whistles are used, these merely call attention to the colored shapes, which are the official starting signals. The race committee sights straight down the line, which is perpendicular to the wind; and any boat that noses over before the countdown reaches zero must return to restart or suffer a penalty.

From Norway with love, the Knarr. In the Oslofyorden, they pronounce the K.

Another group that can use a little extra space is the Predicted Log Racing Association, whose member craft (motorboats for the most part) can be identified by the "PLRA Racer" banners they carry. Despite the misnomer "race," PLRA contests more nearly resemble auto rallies. Predicted logging is a test of precise navigation, with the skipper navigating between checkpoints and timing his arrival not by means of boatspeed or the clock, but by engine rpms alone. An observer aboard carries the only clock and records "mark" at checkpoints. Usually run at moderate speeds, predicted logging demands very careful timing and attention to course. Practitioners appreciate it to the full when someone can and does offer open water.

The Big-Boat Rule

Ignorance of the Big-Boat Rule has gotten more people into trouble than almost any other day-in, day-out aspect of boating. Newcomers are always exposed to the basics: sail has rights over power, starboard has rights over port, and so on. The Big-Boat Rule is different: it is in part a written rule, in part an unwritten rule. It demands the application of common sense.

One evening, for instance, the yawl *Santana* motored out the San Francisco Marina channel, *put-putting* her way toward open water where she could then hoist sails. Under sail, *Santana* is a lively animal despite her fifty-five feet of solid wooden construction—vintage 1923—which weighs some twenty-five tons. Under power, though, she neither stops nor spins on a dime; she plods. Having just cleared the last dock, *Santana* was still inside the breakwater and motoring about four knots when a Windsurfer doing a good fifteen flew in from left field to try to conquer the same space at the same time. And lost. There came a resounding *whap* on the port quarter of the big boat, then a face looked up from the water and growled, "Thaaaaanks, dammit!"

What was *Santana* to do? Her helmsman had no chance of anticipating, much less avoiding, a more maneuverable and much faster-moving craft. Moreover, *Santana* had very little safe water surrounding. While many motorboats have the wherewithal to stop abruptly, sailboats under power do not; nor do they accelerate or turn quickly.

The Big-Boat Rule usually comes into play in a narrow place where the large boat cannot maneuver safely or effectively, but the small boat can. It is unlawful to interfere with a boat that is restricted to a narrow channel; and at the bottom line, every skipper is obligated by law to try to avoid a collision.

The Coast Guard radar watchers at Vessel Traffic Service on Yerba Buena Island still chuckle about the Windsurfer sailor who telephoned to air a heated complaint about being "almost run down by a tanker." Beneath their laughter, however, is concern that not all boaters on San Francisco Bay understand that tankers measure their turning radii in the thousands of yards and their stopping distances by the mile. (Not to pick on boardsailing. It is merely one part of the boating boom that has brought many new people into the sport and sent them out onto the Bay with a little, dangerous knowledge.)

Sailboats do not always have the right of way. The Big-Boat Rule is based on more than common sense. In the case of commercial shipping, Bay approaches and shipping lanes equal narrow channels, and their navigation—in the same currents that sailors face—is a difficult problem even without the prospect of unpredictable behavior by small boats. Merchant ships pass through this, the oldest harbor on the Pacific Coast, more than nine thousand times a year. They do not have the run of the Bay. They must keep to the channels. Some are too deep to use the South Channel, on the San Francisco side of Alcatraz; instead, these very deep vessels enter and leave through the North Channel, which otherwise is reserved for outbound shipping only. The masters of merchant ships have good reason to avoid close

The Yankee, *vintage 1906, reaches toward Red Rock under spinnaker, a modern addition to her gaff schooner rig.*

encounters with small boats: their careers are jeopardized in any collision, no matter who was at fault.

The commercial seaman has two concerns: to move his ship safely, and to move it quickly and economically. With operation costing tens of thousands of dollars per hour, coming to a halt for the sake of some suicide-bent yachtsman would be unattractive, even if they could stop—*and they cannot*. These moving mountains carry their way for miles even with engines full astern and the helmsman working with might and main to keep the course under control. Those who do not get out of his way will have been plowed into the Lower Forty long before he stops. And even if he did succeed in stopping, a big ship "parked" inside the Bay—at the mercy of the tides—could be placed in danger. Control requires speed.

Shipping in the Bay and the approaches falls under the guidance of the Coast Guard's Vessel Traffic Service. From its station atop Yerba Buena, VTS maintains radio and radar watch over traffic, providing information on weather and sea conditions and the positions of ships. The powerful VTS radar is quite likely to pick up a seventy-footer, unlikely to pick up a twenty-footer, and even less likely to give observers an inkling of what the twenty-footer's plans are. VTS maintains watch on Channel 13 (156.65 MHz FM) and will provide shipping information to the yachtsman.

Keeping watch on Channel 16 (156.8 MHz VHF-FM and 2182 KHz AM) is Coast Guard Group San Francisco, the primary local agency for search and rescue. In many cases of distress, however, the quickest way to get help is from a passing boat. Signals can range from the raising and lowering of arms to the igniting of flares. All boats are required by law to carry distress-signaling devices. Engine failure, running out of gas, and (especially in the South Bay) running aground are the situations to which the Coast Guard is most frequently summoned. The Coasties have a busy time of it, protecting lives and property, and too often they are called upon to aid in situations that good seamanship or

foresight could have avoided. The Coast Guard's role is to aid in distress, not to act as a sort of AAA towing service for those who cannot read gas gauges. Too often, too, a skipper who has a problem but is in no immediate danger will holler "Mayday! Mayday!" over the airwaves, causing unneeded consternation and—if he only knew—embarrassment to himself. If the boat is sinking or if a fire is raging out of control, one truly has a mayday. A message of less urgency should begin with the call "Pan." Or if the situation has gone to the dogs, but there is no real urgency, a simple call to "Coast Guard San Francisco" on either of the calling channels will do.

Among the saddest calls the Coast Guard must answer are those regarding drownings, a type of accident that is nearly always preventable with a life jacket. The cold waters of Northern California work against survival for the person who is trying to keep head above water; curiously enough, however, low temperatures work in favor of someone who has drowned. Sudden contact by the face with water lower than 70 degrees Fahrenheit shuts off blood circulation to most parts of the body, conserving the supply for the heart, lungs, and brain. The brain is where blood circulation is needed most, and a cooled brain needs only a fraction of its normal supply of oxygen—little enough that this conserved flow of blood can supply it. Whales, porpoises, and seals survive under water for long periods thanks to similar mechanisms. Humans have recovered, undamaged, from submersions lasting more than half an hour. *Never give up on a drowning victim.*

It is every boat owner or skipper's sober responsibility to learn cardio-pulmonary resuscitation (CPR) and the proper treatment for shock and hypothermia. It is always right to prevent further heat loss in a drowning or hypothermia victim, but it is not always right to rewarm the victim artificially. There is much to know.

Each boat that sails the Bay should also be rehearsed in recovering someone who has fallen overboard. It sounds easy.

"And when I leap into a pit I leap headlong, heels up. . . ."   Dimitri Karamazov

It absolutely is not. Boats that have lost someone in a strong tide condition have found it difficult to get back to that person. When the water is choppy, breathing is difficult. Add sweaters, foul-weather gear, and boots, and even an expert swimmer will be struggling in a very few minutes. Exertion and the loss of body heat to the water take their toll quickly even on the athlete. A nonswimmer without a life jacket will not have time to think about it. *Throw something that floats.* Ropes sink. And be prepared for a real struggle lifting back aboard the wet, dead weight of a living person who will probably be unable to help.

Ranging: A Basic Skill

It is possible to tell at a glance the state of a current one is sailing across simply by taking a range along two stationary objects, straight ahead or straight behind. If three objects are straight in line, and one of them is your boat, they will stay in line until the boat is turned or a current begins to set the boat off course. A buoy in the water and, beyond it, a tree on a hillside will make an excellent range. If the buoy then appears to be moving to the right, for example, this "range" is indicating that one's boat is being set to the left; if the buoy appears to be moving to the left, the range is indicating that one's boat is being set to the right. (For a dry-run demonstration, set two objects in line on a tabletop and observe this relationship as you move your head from side to side.)

Racing sailors use ranges to spot the position of the starting line—preferably by sighting across the entire line from a position well away, aligning both ends of the line with some more distant object. That object, in conjunction with one end of the line or the other, then becomes the range that is used to determine whether one's boat has crossed the line when the starting gun fires.

Ranges also help tell whether one's boat will cross ahead or behind another in an encounter on the water. Simply sight across the other boat to some stationary landmark; if the other boat is moving ahead of that "range," it will pass ahead. If the other boat is falling behind the range, it will pass behind. If the range is unchanging—a *steady range*—one is on a collision course and must take action according to the rules of the road or the racing rules, whichever apply. If both boats are playing things close under the racing rules, it may be necessary to do one's ranging right from the stern (if one is narrowly crossing ahead of a boat that has the right of way) or right from the bow (if one is taking another boat's stern, but wants to pass as close as possible).

In the case of meeting large ships, extra room should be added for courtesy even when one's boat is clearly crossing ahead. Close under the bow of a freighter is no place to be, and it is guaranteed to provoke some long, loud, irate toots—four or more, the danger signal—from the ship's master. It is unsafe to come close: these big ships disturb the windflow, and they create disturbances in the water: a force of suction right into the hull and propellors.

While at night ships carry the standard red light to port and green light to starboard, they also carry range lights: two white lights raised high above the rest of the ship and visible at much greater distances than the red and green. The after light is higher than the forward light; so by watching these two—and treating them like any other range—the yachting skipper can figure out the ship's course and its bearing relative to his own. Knowing that, the skipper then knows what to give, and when.

What to give, when, and how. We have a complex sport. To be sure, sailing is easy; seamanship, however, is a much broader topic than sailing. How to tie a square knot, how to read the sky, how to hold a grip in rough weather, and (yes) how to cook under way—each enters into the sailor's skills. And where strong currents affect the course, those currents must be known. In few of the world's popular sailing spots does the flow of the water matter as much as it does on San Francisco Bay. To sail the Bay is to become a student, willfully or not, of the tides.

To the Farallones under shortened sail.

III: TIDES AND CURRENTS

*T*HE TIDE IS A REACTION, and the tide is a force. At high tide, water bulges away from the planet, reacting to attractive gravities elsewhere (in its own way, our universe likes itself); thus the oceans rise and fall. Likewise the continents, a tiny bit, but we are not used to seeing things that way.

From a boat, in fact, we do not see the tides at all. We care about them because some of the places we can reach at high tide become too shallow at low tide. We care also because the rising tide—the ocean's reaction to the pull of the moon and sun—becomes a powerful thrust of waters spilling through the Golden Gate. Fast currents develop in San Francisco Bay on the rise and again on the fall. It is then that tide becomes a force.

We can anticipate much of what happens in tidal activity because the tides pass in regular cycles: daily, monthly, yearly, and even the nineteen-year cycle that returns the sun and moon to identical relations in the heavens. The highest tides in the monthly cycle are the twice-monthly *spring tides*, which take their name from the strong, springy effect of moon and sun being aligned and exerting their pulls in concert. The alignment need not be perfect (as it would be in an eclipse) for tides to "spring." Figure 1 illustrates such alignments at the new moon and again at the full. Spring tides occur in both situations and the effect is as great with a full moon as with a new moon: the lines of force act in concert on our rapidly spinning planet. The moon, being closer, counts more than the sun, and the moon's 27.3-day orbit

Figure 1. Tidal response at new moon and full moon. The oval line around the earth indicates the tidal forces developed, which are the same at new and full moon phases. This alignment of lunar and solar gravities—*syzygy*—produces the highest tides of the lunar cycle, the spring tides.

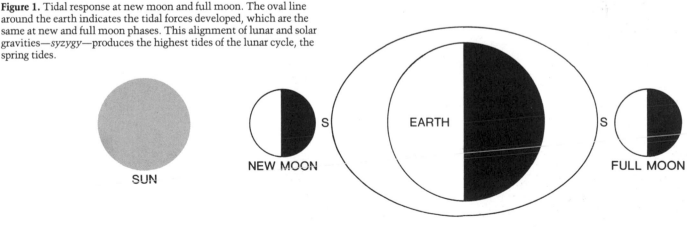

SUN   NEW MOON   S   EARTH   S   FULL MOON

around the earth gives us either a new moon or a full moon—and spring tides—every 13.66 days. Just as spring tides are higher than average at high tide, they are lower at low tide.

After each such peak in its monthly cycle, the moon's continuing orbit brings it out of alignment with the sun; their combined pull becomes less, and the range of the tide (the difference between high and low) lessens. High tides each day are a little lower and low tides each day are a little higher until the moon reaches either first quarter (after the new moon) or third quarter (after the full moon). The earth's primordial satellite and its star are then out of phase just as far as they ever go. They are said to be in *quadrature*, tugging almost at right angles. The tidal response is weakest, and the tidal range is least. This is the period of *neap tides*, as shown in figure 2. After each such low point in the monthly cycle, the moon's path draws it once again closer to alignment with the sun. Each day, high tides rise a little higher and low tides fall a little lower until moon and sun are aligned, and tides again spring to high highs and low lows.

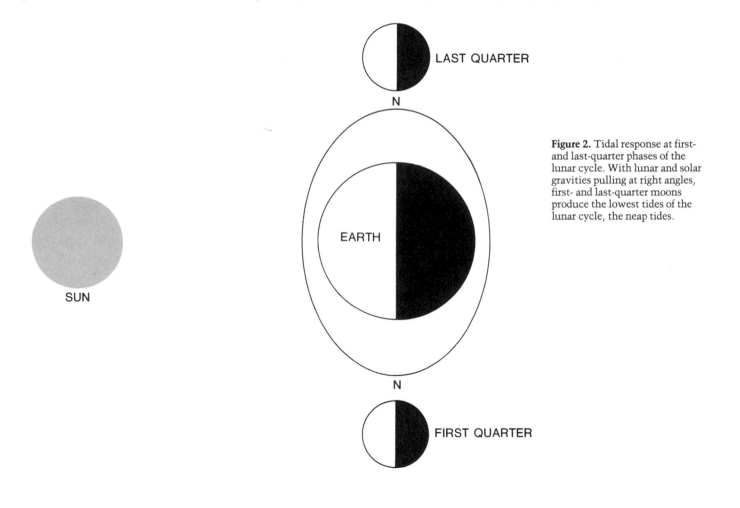

Figure 2. Tidal response at first- and last-quarter phases of the lunar cycle. With lunar and solar gravities pulling at right angles, first- and last-quarter moons produce the lowest tides of the lunar cycle, the neap tides.

There is also a time in each lunar orbit when the moon is at *perigee*—as near earth as it comes—and draws high *perigean* tides simply by being so close. A perigean tide may temporarily interrupt a trend in the monthly cycle, as when the moon at perigee raises the level of a neap tide. When two or more high-tide events transpire at the same time, tides frequently creep higher than they would due to either factor alone. If a winter storm also happens to be under way, it becomes a winter to remember. Richardson Bay swells across the mud flats, dampening almost the very doors of the Tamalpais High gymnasium in Mill Valley. The South Bay spreads so far the marshlands are unrecognizable. While the storm is blowing, egrets hold their feathers close and do not forage long.

Tides on San Francisco Bay occur in two cycles daily: there are two highs and two lows. Such tides are called *semidiurnal*. The two highs are usually very different in height, as are the two lows. Thus we have the terms *higher high water* and *lower high water, lower low water* and *higher low water.* At oceanfront locations in Northern California, the average difference between high tides on a given day is two feet; the average difference between lows is two to three feet—which is one of the reasons the level of *mean lower low water* is taken as the reference point for water depths printed on Pacific Coast charts. The makers of tide books take the same cue, giving height of tides as so many feet above or below mean lower low water. The mean tidal range—the average difference between high- and low-water marks—is four feet at the Golden Gate; the maximum range is about nine feet.

At 13.66-day intervals, the moon arrives at a point overhead either the Tropic of Cancer or the Tropic of Capricorn, the farthest respective reach of its north–south transit. At this, its maximum declination (angle to equator), the moon causes maximum difference between the day's two highs and two lows: Tropic Tides. Passing between the Tropic of Cancer and the Tropic of Capricorn, the moon crosses the equator, drawing as it does the least difference between highs and lows: Equatorial Tides. Occasionally a twenty-four-hour day sees only three peaks of the total cycle; but when that happens, the next tide will follow hard on the heels of midnight. A complete tidal day is 24.84 hours. No part of the tidal cycle is ever lost; low tide will not be followed by another low tide.

If the actual workings of tidal activity were as simple as our illustrations have been, we would need tide books much less than we do. But our illustrations are simplified for the sake of making certain points and do not show the other influences afoot. Figure 1, for example, shows the positions of sun and moon at the time spring tides are generated; but the tide response itself is actually somewhat delayed: high tide does not occur while the moon is directly overhead (this fact has been recognized since at least the first century A.D. Our first writing comes from Pliny the Elder of Rome, who was hard put to explain what we now call the *lunitidal interval*). In the spring tide's lunitidal interval, a day or more passes before the waters react with a maximum tide to the moon and sun's alignment. In the latest thinking, the main cause of this delay is inertia: water has mass, mass has inertia, and inertia slows response time.

In stages intermediate between neap tide and spring tide, there is a period when high-tide forces are developed before the moon's passage overhead. Figure 3, which again ignores delays in response time, illustrates this situation. While the moon exerts a much greater pull than the sun on the earth's waters, the sun plays a role in generating tides; and the tidal bulge appears somewhere between their nearest points on the planet.

As the moon orbits the earth, it moves in the same direction the earth rotates. A complete lunar orbit takes 27.3 earth rotations. This rotation being much faster than the moon's apparent speed in its orbiting path, we can understand another phenomenon of the tides. The tidal cycle runs about fifty minutes later each day. Why? As the world turns, it allows the San Francisco Bay, or any point on the planet, to "catch up" with the moon's overhead position fifty minutes later each day.

We now have enough pieces of the puzzle to think about tides the way scientists do. There are other causes of the lunitidal interval. Look again at figure 3 and think of the moon rotating slowly through its orbit and the earth rotating relatively quickly. The earth in fact is turning while the tidal bulges stand still, in a sense. Oceanographers speak of the bulge as a tide wave (not to be confused with the catastrophe-induced tsunami, or "tidal wave"). These tide waves have an apparent motion across the face of a planet; to be more precise, the planet is turning beneath them.

Nothing in the mathematics of tidal theory says these waves could not travel at more than a thousand miles per hour, at a speed equivalent to the moon's apparent speed around a rotating planet; but they could do so only in very deep, unobstructed waters. As it is, the ocean depths vary and the tide waves are obstructed by islands and continents. Tidal effects consequently vary in different oceans and in different parts of the same ocean, the actual speed of the tide wave not exceeding 750 miles per hour. The tide wave moves as a forced wave; its position relative to the moon rides on a balance between the attraction of sun and moon and friction with the ocean bottom.

It is rare to be able to isolate a single tidal effect and assign it to a single causative force. So it is with *diurnal inequality*, the difference between the two highs and the two lows of any given day, whose principal cause is the tilt of the earth on its axis. Figure 4 tells this part of the story, in a period of new moon. Backlighted, with its dark face toward earth, the moon is nearly invisible. The arrows in the northern hemisphere illustrate the direction of tidal flow. Waters in the southern hemisphere respond in kind. Response delays

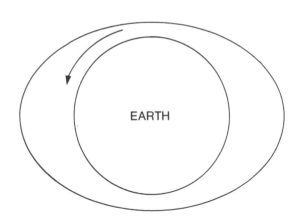

MOON

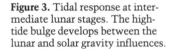

Figure 3. Tidal response at intermediate lunar stages. The high-tide bulge develops between the lunar and solar gravity influences.

SUN

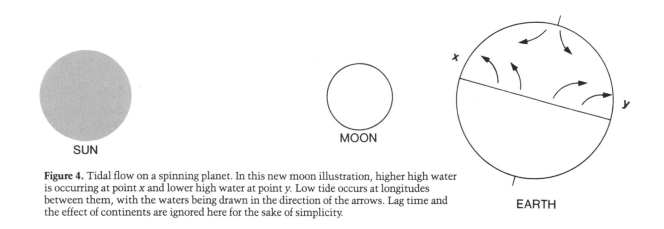

SUN

MOON

EARTH

Figure 4. Tidal flow on a spinning planet. In this new moon illustration, higher high water is occurring at point *x* and lower high water at point *y*. Low tide occurs at longitudes between them, with the waters being drawn in the direction of the arrows. Lag time and the effect of continents are ignored here for the sake of simplicity.

are ignored, also the interference of continents. At the moment shown, tidal forces act with greatest strength at point x. Twelve hours later, the rotating planet brings point x to point y. There will be another high tide, but not as high, because the forces are less (low tides are meanwhile occurring along longitudes at right angles to the lunar–solar pull). At point y the combined forces of moon and sun act more upon rock than water, more upon land than sea. The spinning of the planet creates a centrifugal force wanting to fling the waters outward, even while moon and sun are drawing the land toward them—a land tide. This mix of forces produces a lower high tide (and then a higher low tide) on the dark side of the planet.

On a more local scale of influence is the Coriolus force. Created by the earth's rotation, its effect bends all forces to the right in the Northern Hemisphere. One will never notice it from a yacht, but the Coriolus force may cause the flood tide on the south shore of the Golden Gate to rise a couple centimeters higher than on the north shore.

Atmospheric weight is another and important variable. Air pressure averages 14.7 pounds per square inch at sea level, but that weight varies with temperature and other factors. In winter storms, a variation of as much as a foot in water level is entirely possible due to changes in atmos-

pheric pressure. A strong westerly driving the surface of a flood tide in summertime may raise water levels by a foot over calm conditions and delay the turn of the tide by nearly half an hour. Rivers too rise and fall, changing the flow of the water. So it is that not only a tide book, but a measure of judgment as well, must inform tidal strategy.

Tides account for about 80 percent of the variability of currents on San Francisco Bay. That leaves a strapping 20 percent for the influence of river flow, prevailing or perverse wind, atmospheric pressure, and spirits unnameable by day. The last local survey of tides and currents was made in 1980 by the NOAA ship *MacArthur*. An officer of the *MacArthur* commented at the end of the survey that he had used the tide books for the sake of deploying instrument buoys at minimum current. The books were accurate, he believed, "Give or take half an hour."

Fortunately the semi-empirical approach to tide theory works wonders. The largely reliable predictions of tide books are developed from the data of past years in combination with the Equilibrium Model and its three principal factors related to sun and moon: changes in declination (angle to the earth's equator); changes in distance from earth; and changes in relative position.

When the staff members of the National Oceanic and

Atmospheric Administration (NOAA) sit down in their Rockville, Maryland offices to work out the tide books for San Francisco Bay, they make liberal use of a bank of computers. Taking the permutations of the changing positions of sun, moon, and earth, as many as sixty-two tidal constituents may be used to make predictions. The response to each constituent is considered a partial tide. The actual tide then equals the sum of these parts, weighed against the effect of river discharge at a particular time of the year, as predicted from the data of previous years.

Push Comes to Shove

In this mix of theory and empirical experience, theory works rather well for predicting tides at ocean ports, where the rebound of the tide wave—bouncing off the continent—

Of Aristotle, Galileo, and Newton

The relative importance of these factors—even the existence of "land tides"—and other factors unnamed here are matters of controversy in the halls of academe. The experts quibble, and the last well-chosen word has not been written. An ancient legend had it that Aristotle died distraught, a suicide, hurling himself into the rushing waters of the Euripe because he could not explain the movement of the tides. Historians do not accept the story, but it must have seemed plausible to the perplexed generations that succeeded Aristotle. Accustomed to waters where tidal effects were scarcely noticeable, the author of *The Poetics* spent the last few months of his life on the island of Euboea, separated from mainland Greece by the Euripe. In this narrow channel, tidal exchanges between Aegean and Mediterranean waters stimulate currents as great as nine knots.

Babylonian philosophers, secure behind their figured walls and bronze gates, theorized that the moon in passing compressed the atmosphere, which compressed the waters, which generated tides. Long after, no less a seventeenth-century rationalist than René Descartes carried on this notion, cogitating a space filled with ether. On the boot of Italy, Galileo Galilei's own seventeenth-century mind was set on showing the earth to be round, and orbiting the sun, and rotating on its axis. Tidal action he blamed on the ocean's inability to keep pace. Galileo compared tides to the sloshing of waters in a big bowl. He offered this as further proof that the world turned, and the pooh-poohed anyone who suggested maybe the moon attracted water.

Galileo died in 1642, the year Isaac Newton was born. Forty-five years later, Newton's *Philophae Naturalis Principia Mathematica* was published, giving us our present understanding of tidal action in the process of giving us the concept of gravity. From Newton we understand why the moon exerts more force than the sun, even though the sun is much larger: gravitational attraction increases in direct proportion to the square of mass and decreases in proportion to the cube of distance. So while the sun has much more inherent gravity, the tiny moon has nearly twice the influence because its distance from the earth averages only 238,855 miles; the sun, on the other hand, is 93 million miles away. (Of course, the earth's own gravity places the greatest force upon itself. The cumulative effect of moon and sun, in one popular estimation, is only one nine-millionth of earth's gravity.)

It rains a lot in England, so Newton had time to think on these things. If his picture of tidal behavior is not simple, it is at least easier to hold in the mind than anything offered in our own century by Albert is relatively uncomplicated. Inside the San Francisco Bay and Delta, experience plays a larger hand: the tide wave bounds and rebounds from crooks and islands and shallows. It meets the flow of sixteen rivers and, all together, they play some pretty tricks. While sailors really need not cure themselves of casually saying, "The tide is coming in," or "The tide is going out," they should at least be aware of the technical inaccuracy. Tides rise and fall. A rising tide is a *flood tide*. A falling tide is an *ebb tide*. The rise and fall help stir horizontal movements of water called *current*. Flood currents flow into the Bay. Ebb currents flow out.

One-sixth of the volume of the Bay flows out (and in) with each tide cycle. Because the ebb is reinforced with river water, ebb currents tend to flow a little longer and stronger than flood currents. A pattern of 7s and 5s—seven hours of ebb for five hours of flood—is knocked about as a rule of thumb, but it is far from gospel. On the rise, flood tide will affect the waterways all the way to Sacramento: not by carrying ocean water that far, but by effectively damming the rivers and pushing the water level up. Thus the tide wave advances, moving with its greatest force through the deepest cuts.

What once were the stream beds of ancient rivers are now the deep-water shipping channels of the Bay—one hundred feet deep between Alcatraz and Angel islands, forty feet deep beneath the Richmond–San Rafael Bridge. These same channels bear the strongest currents on the flood and again on the ebb. In the shallows that comprise most of the Bay, there is much less movement of water. High tide becomes the upshot of water piling up against water; this is especially noticeable in the South Bay, where current charts show no velocity arrows outside the channels.

Science calls a region of mingling fresh and salt waters an estuary. About one-fifth of the San Francisco Bay estuary is fresh water, and the ways and means of its mixing dictate much of the ecology. The point of greatest saltwater penetration—the *null zone*—lies a few miles inland from Carquinez Strait, advancing or retreating with decreasing or increasing river flow. Because there is a net change of water over a number of tidal cycles in the main body of the Bay, a raft floating on San Pablo Bay will drift out and in a bit with each tidal cycle, but each ebb will carry it closer to the Gate until, eventually, the raft checks out and goes to sea.

The misnamed "Oakland Estuary" is actually the shipping channel of Oakland Harbor, a cut near the northern

Einstein, who wanted to relieve us entirely of the concept of gravity (the most troublesome component of Newton's Equilibrium Theory) so that we could inhabit instead a space–time continuum curved around a magnetic field. Who can say what comfort curved space might have been to Newton, rubbing his apple-bumped head, as he wrote, "Hitherto we have explained the phenomena of the heavens and of our sea by the power of gravity, but . . . I have not been able to discover the cause of these properties from phenomena, and I frame no hypothesis."

Newton was well aware that his mathematics left unexplained gaps in the behavior of tides. Tides are touched by many more subtle influences than can be accounted for by our simplified picture of a "traveling bulge." The earth, for example, does not rotate around its core; rather, the earth and moon revolve around a common center of gravity lying a thousand miles below the earth's surface and some three thousand miles from its center, a fact that now leads astronomers to think of the earth and moon as a binary planet system rather than as planet and satellite. If the moon is powerful enough to weave the earth through its orbit around the sun, it should come as no surprise that the moon acts upon the waters. The "friction" of the tides in turn acts upon the moon, apparently allowing it to slip further from the earth.

extremity of the South Bay. Because the South Bay has very little freshwater drainage of its own, it depends on flow from the north (through San Pablo Bay) for its daily and seasonal "flush": waters are exchanged between North Bay and South Bay for a period during each change of the tide. As the ebb weakens but before the flood reaches strength, waters flow into the South Bay. Current charts show this clearly, though without even hinting how we should name a cur-

rent that is ebbing from here and flooding to there (a flebb?). For a South Bay that receives much more than its share of sewage and industrial waste from cities surrounding, this influx from the North Bay is the only effective cleansing action—and one of the reasons some minds fear any further reduction of river flow into the estuary.

A general understanding of current and eddy, combined with information available from tide books and current charts, can resolve the principal questions of small boat travel: is the water deep enough? will the currents help or hinder? Finer points matter only to the racing set, who have seen it proved over and over that when it comes to the finer points, there is no substitute for applied intelligence. Expert racing sailors from other parts of the world often win races on San Francisco Bay in spite of the "local knowledge advantage." Equipped with a general feel for how currents flow and tides turn, they check the turf, then get down to business. Having observed a few top competitors developing tidal strategy, I can report that they will check the tide book, then *look at the water*, and draw their conclusions from what they see. They treat the tide book as a resource, the Bay as truth.

The Most Misread Book in Town

Tide books differ slightly in what they offer, but they have certain basics in common. Any tide book will include a daily calendar for a given year, January 1 through December 31, and will indicate the phases of the moon. For each day it will state times for high and low water; it will also list those tidal heights in feet above or below mean lower low water, giving similar information for currents. Somewhere in the front of the tide book will appear a statement informing the reader that all figures are approximate.

Our references in this chapter will be the tide tables for April 1981 shown in table 1. Times and heights apply to the Golden Gate. In the left column of the tides table are the

Table 1

TIDES AT SAN FRANCISCO (Golden Gate), CALIFORNIA — 1981
Pacific Daylight Saving Time Starts Sun., April 26th* (Heights in feet)

APRIL									
MOON PHASES	Day	Time	Ht.	Time	Ht.	Time	Ht.	Time	Ht.
		Lo Water		Hi Water		Lo Water		Hi Water	
	Wed. 1	0227	2.0	0827	5.3	1449	−0.4	2153	4.9
	Thu. 2	0311	1.4	0923	5.4	1532	−0.4	2227	5.2
Equa. NEW Perigee	Fri. 3	0355	0.7	1015	5.5	1614	−0.3	2259	5.4
	Sat. 4	0436	0.1	1109	5.5	1656	0.0	2334	5.7
	Sun. 5	0525	−0.4	1204	5.3	1735	0.4	- - -	- -
		Hi Water		Lo Water		Hi Water		Lo Water	
	Mon. 6	0010	5.9	0611	−0.7	1300	5.1	1820	1.0
	Tue. 7	0051	6.0	0703	−0.8	1402	4.8	1907	1.5
No. Equa. FIRST Q.	Wed. 8	0134	6.0	0758	−0.8	1509	4.6	2001	2.1
	Thu. 9	0224	5.9	0901	−0.6	1624	4.5	2107	2.5
	Fri. 10	0322	5.6	1007	−0.4	1744	4.5	2229	2.7
	Sat. 11	0424	5.4	1118	−0.2	1853	4.6	2353	2.6
	Sun. 12	0541	5.1	1226	−0.1	1954	4.8	- - -	- -
		Lo Water		Hi Water		Lo Water		Hi Water	
	Mon. 13	0106	2.3	0653	5.0	1325	0.0	2041	5.0
	Tue. 14	0204	1.8	0759	4.9	1418	0.1	2120	5.1
	Wed. 15	0254	1.4	0858	4.9	1500	0.2	2155	5.2
Equa. FULL Apogee	Thu. 16	0336	0.9	0950	4.8	1539	0.4	2226	5.2
	Fri. 17	0412	0.6	1037	4.7	1614	0.7	2254	5.2
	Sat. 18	0447	0.3	1121	4.5	1646	1.0	2318	5.1
	Sun. 19	0519	0.1	1204	4.4	1717	1.4	2344	5.1
	Mon. 20	0554	0.0	1246	4.3	1749	1.8	- - -	- -
		Hi Water		Lo Water		Hi Water		Lo Water	
	Tue. 21	0007	5.1	0630	−0.1	1332	4.2	1821	2.2
	Wed. 22	0034	5.1	0705	−0.1	1418	4.1	1857	2.6
	Thu. 23	0105	5.1	0744	0.0	1514	4.0	1939	2.9
So. Equa.	Fri. 24	0144	5.0	0829	0.1	1613	4.0	2033	3.1
	Sat. 25	0233	4.8	0925	0.1	1722	4.0	2147	3.2
	Sun. 26	0428	4.7	1125	0.2	1921	4.2	- - -	- -
		Lo Water		Hi Water		Lo Water		Hi Water	
LAST Q.	Mon. 27	0011	3.1	0534	4.5	1225	0.1	2010	4.4
	Tue. 28	0121	2.7	0647	4.5	1325	0.0	2051	4.7
	Wed. 29	0215	2.1	0759	4.5	1418	0.0	2130	4.9
	Thu. 30	0304	1.4	0908	4.6	1507	0.0	2205	5.3

phases of the moon, showing on April 4 a new moon (aligned with the sun's gravity and applying the tandem pull that draws spring tides). On April 5 the moon reached its closest orbiting point to earth; it was at perigee. Allowing for some lag time due to inertia, the combination of new moon and perigee would lead us to expect some very high and low tides to follow; on April 7 and 8 we find the highest and lowest tides of the month. Higher high water both days was predicted to rise 6.0 feet above mean lower low water at the Golden Gate. The time on April 7 was 12:51 P.M. for high tide, and on April 8, 1:34 P.M. or 43 minutes later (remembering our 50-minute average). In the low water column, the minus sign leading the number (−0.8 feet in this case) tells that water levels dropped below mean lower low water. The *tidal range*—the difference between high and low—was 6.8 feet. Notice that highs were not as high and lows were not as low in the tidal cycle that followed—unequal tides as usual.

Gone with the wind is the day when old Fort Point could be considered a guardian of the Bay's approaches. Its brick battlements survive for sightseers in the shade of the Golden Gate Bridge, and the Fort's location in the narrow mouth of the strait—seven-tenths of a mile wide—becomes point zero in tabulating tide and current differences in the region, nearby ocean ports included (the high and low figures in table 1 apply only at the Golden Gate). It takes time for the tide wave to travel.

The rising tide in the Golden Gate has a battle to fight before it may crest. It must halt the ebb and turn it back—a tough job, but the ocean gets it done. As a path of least resistance, it certainly beats pushing back the bluffs at Muir Beach.

Inside the estuary, the movement of the tide wave is complex. It has different characteristics in different areas. The range through which tides fluctuate is a large portion—24 percent—of the total volume of the Bay, which averages only eighteen feet deep at mean lower low water. A progressive wave propagates through the North Bay, originating in the cresting wave that floods through the Golden Gate. Due to river flow, tide levels at high water are slightly higher in the North Bay than elsewhere, and low tides on the average do not fall as far: the tidal range is the least in the estuary. The progressive wave of the North Bay flood tide disappears in each cycle and is renewed with the next flooding turn of the tide.

Tides in the South Bay behave very differently: a standing wave oscillates back and forth, north and south, much like the sloshing of waters in a bowl. It moves more quickly than the progressive wave of the North Bay, causing high tide to appear sooner in the South than in the North Bay, even at points the same distance from the Golden Gate. As this standing wave oscillates, it creates the largest range of tide within the estuary—half again the range at the Golden Gate.

This oscillation is bound up with the action of the "flebb," which always occurs during the transition between tidal cycles, at about the time of slack water at the Golden Gate. At the end of the ebb, for example, the South Bay reaches low water sooner than the North Bay—while flood tide forces are beginning to stem the ebb flow in the Golden Gate but before they reach real strength. The North Bay is still ebbing and the South Bay is ready to rise. Outward flow through the Gate has slowed, so the North Bay ebb flows into the South Bay. A similar process occurs at the change from flood to ebb. The South Bay, which has already seen the cresting of the tide, ebbs into the North Bay.

Traveling times for the tide wave show dramatically in the Table of Differences and Constants, table 2, which is zero-based at Fort Point. The ocean port of Half Moon Bay sees the crest of the flood tide one hour, 10 minutes sooner than Fort Point; that is given as a reading of −1.10. Other ocean fronts likewise see high water ahead of the Golden Gate.

For points inside the Bay, the minus signs turn to plusses,

indicating the delay in the crest of the tide. At the San Mateo Bridge in the South Bay, the delay waiting for high tide is 39 minutes, given as a reading of +39. At Sacramento, eighty-one nautical miles upriver, the delay is seven hours, 30 minutes, +7.30.

It would be convenient if the time differences for high water matched the time differences for low water, but nature's mathematics are not so simple. Half Moon Bay sees low tide sooner than Fort Point by 56 minutes. The difference at the San Mateo Bridge is a delay of one hour, 14 minutes. Between Fort Point and Sacramento, the delay is nine hours, 29 minutes.

Accompanying the time differences in table 2 are height differences given as a ratio. Among different points, the height of the tide varies as much as the timing. At ocean-front locations—Monterey, Santa Cruz, Half Moon Bay, and the San Francisco Bay—low-water levels agree with those at Fort Point. This is the ocean, just doing its thing.

In the Golden Gate, however, high-water levels push higher as they near Fort Point. Here, current meets current; we no longer have a "pure" tide. Pinched in the narrows, the incoming tide wave rises. Inside the Bay it meets the ebb and turns it around, pressing up water levels. High-tide marks are higher at Alcatraz than Fort Point though a mere 2.6 miles of Bay water run between them. The height-difference ratio for Alcatraz is +0.1, giving a higher high-water height on April 7 of $0.1 \times 6.0 = 0.6$; $6.0 + 0.6 = 6.6$ feet above mean lower low water. That is over half a foot of height difference in very little distance.

At the foot of San Francisco's Mission Street, the ratio is +0.3. In the South Bay at Hunters Point, the ratio is a whopping 0.9, giving a reading in the wee morning hours of April 7 of $0.9 \times 6.0 = 5.4$; $6.0 + 5.4 = 11.4$ feet above mean lower low water. Set out with a fast motor from the Golden Gate at high tide and time yourself to reach Hunters Point thirty minutes later; your boat will have traveled 5.4 feet *uphill*.

Flood-tide pile-up is as visible—and busier—to the north. At Point Richmond, high tide is delayed 36 minutes with a height ratio of +0.2. On the San Joaquin River at Antioch (near the null zone, between fresh river water and the mixed salt/fresh composite of the Bay), high tides come three hours, 56 minutes later than at the Golden Gate. The level

Table 2
TIDAL DIFFERENCES AND OTHER CONSTANTS

| | DIFFERENCES | | | |
| | Time | | Heights | |
PLACE	High water	Low water	High water	Low water
Monterey—Monterey Bay	−1.16	−0.58	−0.5	0.0
Santa Cruz	−1.19	−1.04	−0.5	0.0
Half Moon Bay	−1.10	−0.56	−0.2	0.0
San Francisco Bar	−0.39	−0.37	−0.1	0.0
San Francisco (Golden Gate)	—	—	—	—
Alcatraz Island	+0.10	+0.12	+0.1	0.0
San Francisco, North Point	+0.15	+0.22	+0.1	0.0
San Francisco, Mission Street	+0.27	+0.36	+0.3	0.0
Oakland Pier	+0.29	+0.42	+0.3	0.0
Alameda	+0.34	+0.46	+0.7	0.0
Oakland Harbor, Grove Street	+0.29	+0.36	+0.5	0.0
Potrero Point	+0.29	+0.40	+0.6	0.0
Point Avisadero, Hunters Point	+0.30	+0.43	+0.9	0.0
San Mateo Bridge	+0.39	+1.14	+1.9	+0.1
Redwood Creek Entrance (inside)	+1.02	+1.32	+2.2	+0.1
Dumbarton Highway Bridge	+0.48	+1.27	+2.7	+0.1
Alviso (bridge) Alviso Slough	+1.20	+2.18	+3.3	+0.1
Sausalito	+0.09	+0.13	−0.2	0.0
Angel Island (east side)	+0.22	+0.33	0.0	0.0
Richmond	+0.21	+0.29	+0.1	0.0
Point Richmond	+0.36	+0.40	+0.2	0.0
Point Orient	+0.47	+0.54	+0.1	0.0
Point San Quentin (San Pablo Bay)	+0.46	+0.58	0.0	0.0
McNear	+1.05	+1.07	+0.1	0.0
Pinole Point	+1.19	+1.32	+0.4	0.0
Hercules	+1.26	+1.53	+0.4	0.0
Petaluma Creek Entrance	+1.15	+2.15	+0.5	0.0
Selby	+1.25	+1.58	+0.7	0.0
Vallejo, Mare Island Strait	+1.41	+2.04	+0.4	−0.1
Napa, Napa River	+2.12	+2.46	+1.5	0.0
Crockett	+1.54	+2.16	+0.3	−0.1
Benicia, Army Point	+1.57	+2.23	+0.3	0.0
Port Chicago	+2.30	+3.14	−0.2	−0.1
Pittsburg, New York Slough	+3.23	+4.13	−1.1	−0.4
Point Buckler	+2.36	+3.18	−0.2	−0.3
Suisun Slough Entrance	+2.45	+3.27	−0.3	−0.3
Antioch	+3.56	+4.42	*0.74	*0.55
Three Mile Slough Entrance	+4.50	+5.48	*0.61	*0.45
Prisoners Point	+5.49	+6.39	*0.61	*0.45
Wards Island	+6.08	+7.02	*0.63	*0.45
Black Slough Landing	+6.24	+7.23	*0.67	*0.45
Stockton	+6.45	+7.47	*0.71	*0.45
Sacramento	+7.30	+9.29	*0.51	*0.27
Bolinas Bay	−0.29	−0.17	0.0	0.0
Point Reyes	−1.05	−0.37	0.0	+0.1
Tomales Bay Entrance	−0.16	+0.10	*0.88	*0.91
Bodega Head Entrance	−0.42	−0.22	−0.1	+0.1
Point Arena	−0.46	−0.27	0.0	0.0

*Ratio: The Height of Water from Main Reference Point Table must be multiplied by ratio given to determine Height of High or Low water for these subordinate stations.

is higher by a factor of 0.74. River flow has its say: it keeps low-water marks here higher than at the Gate by a factor of +0.55. The figures for Antioch and points upriver are preceded by an asterisk, meaning they apply only during low-river stages. If the streams are swollen from spring snowmelt in the Sierra, or if the river is low from drought, the ratios do not hold.

We have based our discussion on the sort of pocket-edition tide books found in cuddies and bilges of most Northern California yachts. These pocket editions are handy, adequate for many uses, and—best of all—they are given away by marine stores. Much more detailed information can be gained from government publications, including the Department of Commerce's *Tide Tables for the Pacific Coast of North America and Asia* and a separate book of *Tidal Current Tables* for the same. Also useful is the *Coast Pilot for the Pacific Coast: California, Oregon, Washington, and Hawaii*. The first two books contain tables and very little text. The *Coast Pilot* contains a great deal of text describing tide and current activity, weather patterns, and prominent land features for aid in navigation.

For those whose interest is regional, and who want to avoid the expense of books whose treatment of Iloilo Strait in the Philippines is just as thorough as their treatment of the Golden Gate, much of the same material is reproduced in almanacs with a narrower focus. Besides tidal information, almanacs include safety information, light and radio beacon lists, and a harbor guide.

The *Coast Pilot* and the almanacs also deal in currents—a matter of more urgency to sailors, in most cases, than the rise and fall of the tide. When San Francisco sailors say, "Check the tide book," they usually mean, "Check the currents." Maximum flood current and maximum ebb current are the benchmarks for nearly all the figuring we do on how to sail the Bay. Max flood does not coincide with high water, nor does max ebb coincide with low water—or even with the most rapid change in vertical height—so we are blessed with separate tables for currents, also for current differences and constants.

For our example of April 7, table 3 reveals that the new moon—near perigee, drawing the highest and lowest tides of the month—also stirred some of the strongest currents. A 5.2-knot ebb current at the Golden Gate followed the +6.0-foot higher-high-water reading. By contrast, the last-quarter moon of April 27 (tugging at right angles to the gravity of the sun) drew only a +4.5-foot higher-high-water reading, fol-

Table 3

CURRENT TABLES
SAN FRANCISCO BAY ENTRANCE (Golden Gate) CALIF., 1981
f — flood, direction 65° true.   e — ebb, direction 245° true.

APRIL   Pacific Daylight Saving Time Starts Sun., April 26th*

(Time in h.m.; Velocity in kn.)

Day	Slack Water Time	Max. Current Time Vel.
1 W	0447, 1025, 1717, 2329	0116 2.8e, 0734 2.8f, 1329 4.4e, 2017 3.8f
2 Th	0530, 1117, 1758	0201 3.4e, 0820 3.4f, 1417 4.7e, 2056 4.1f
3 F	0005, 0613, 1208, 1838	0244 4.1e, 0906 3.9f, 1504 4.8e, 2134 4.2f
4 Sa	0040, 0657, 1300, 1918	0327 4.6e, 0952 4.2f, 1551 4.7e, 2212 4.2f
5 Su	0116, 0743, 1353, 2000	0410 5.0e, 1041 4.4f, 1637 4.4e, 2253 3.9f
6 M	0153, 0831, 1449, 2043	0457 5.2e, 1131 4.4f, 1725 3.9e, 2338 3.6f
7 Tu	0232, 0925, 1549, 2131	0542 5.2e, 1226 4.1f, 1814 3.2e
8 W	0316, 1024, 1653, 2227	0023 3.1f, 0632 5.0e, 1324 3.8f, 1911 2.6e

Day	Slack Water Time	Max. Current Time Vel.
9 Th	0407, 1129, 1803, 2338	0118 2.5f, 0727 4.6e, 1432 3.4f, 2009 2.1e
10 F	0509, 1240, 1915	0218 2.1f, 0828 4.1e, 1553 3.2f, 2123 1.7e
11 Sa	0100, 0621, 1351, 2022	0335 1.8f, 0936 3.8e, 1714 3.2f, 2301 1.8e
12 Su	0219, 0736, 1457, 2120	0503 1.9f, 1055 3.6e, 1817 3.3f
13 M	0325, 0847, 1554, 2208	0032 2.1e, 0617 2.2f, 1209 3.6e, 1911 3.5f
14 Tu	0420, 0949, 1643, 2249	0125 2.6e, 0716 2.6f, 1313 3.7e, 1954 3.6f
15 W	0508, 1044, 1726, 2326	0200 3.0e, 0805 3.0f, 1356 3.7e, 2033 3.6f
16 Th	0549, 1133, 1805, 2359	0229 3.4e, 0846 3.2f, 1433 3.7e, 2106 3.5f

Day	Slack Water Time	Max. Current Time Vel.
17 F	0628, 1218, 1841	0253 3.7e, 0927 3.4f, 1506 3.6e, 2135 3.4f
18 Sa	0030, 0704, 1301, 1914	0322 3.9e, 1000 3.5f, 1538 3.4e, 2200 3.2f
19 Su	0059, 0739, 1343, 1945	0354 4.1e, 1034 3.5f, 1615 3.2e, 2230 2.9f
20 M	0127, 0813, 1425, 2014	0427 4.2e, 1106 3.4f, 1650 2.9e, 2259 2.6f
21 Tu	0153, 0849, 1508, 2043	0502 4.2e, 1145 3.2f, 1729 2.6e, 2334 2.3f
22 W	0221, 0927, 1555, 2114	0541 4.1e, 1226 3.0f, 1810 2.2e
23 Th	0251, 1011, 1647, 2152	0015 2.0f, 0624 3.9e, 1311 2.7f, 1858 1.9e
24 F	0328, 1102, 1746, 2246	0058 1.7f, 0711 3.7e, 1406 2.5f, 1949 1.6e

Day	Slack Water Time	Max. Current Time Vel.
25 Sa	0415, 1201, 1848	0149 1.4f, 0806 3.4e, 1503 2.4f, 2048 1.5e
*26 Su	0107, 0618, 1405, 2048	0355 1.2f, 1002 3.3e, 1711 2.5f, 2253 1.6e
27 M	0235, 0735, 1506, 2142	0502 1.3f, 1103 3.3e, 1814 2.7f, 2355 1.9e
28 Tu	0343, 0854, 1602, 2228	0613 1.6f, 1200 3.5e, 1909 3.1f
29 W	0439, 1004, 1652, 2310	0053 2.5e, 0714 2.2f, 1303 3.7e, 1957 3.4f
30 Th	0527, 1107, 1739, 2348	0147 3.2e, 0812 2.9f, 1359 4.0e, 2038 3.8f

lowed by a 3.3-knot ebb. Listed to the left of the time column for maximum current are the times for *slack water*, which should be understood as a brief turnaround in the Golden Gate—not a period of quiescence throughout the Bay.

The National Ocean Survey and NOAA publish a set of widely reproduced current charts for the San Francisco Bay. There are twelve charts in all, one for each hour of the twice-daily cycle. NOAA's information is drawn in broad strokes but is fairly accurate. If you want to sail from one point to another, the charts tell very well what to expect; for a cruise or a quick joyride, there is nothing more to ask. Those who luxuriate in traveling without a time schedule may even find transcendent moods to stemming a foul current uncaring, since the day is all there is and the sailing is all there will be.

Then, alas, there is the race. The race-minded really do want to know whether to take that extra fifty-yard tack in

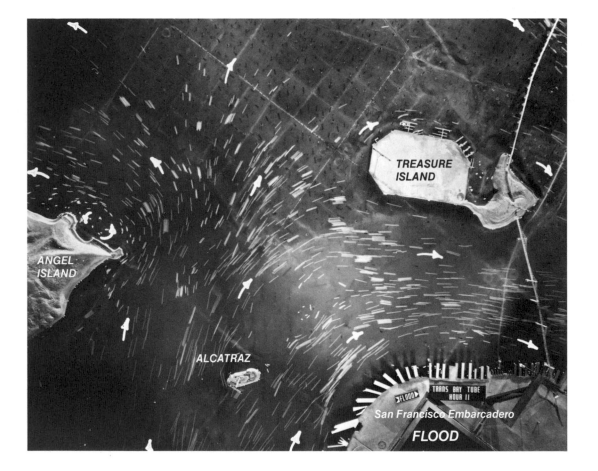

Flood tide

Flood tide as photographed in the Army Corps of Engineers Bay Model in Sausalito. On model time, the photograph was taken one hour after maximum flood. The Delta's net outflow equals 16,000 cubic feet per second. Surface current direction is shown by the streaks made by confetti in a four-second exposure. A one-eighth-inch streak indicates a current velocity of one foot per second. A five-eighths-inch streak indicates a current velocity of five feet per second. Note the protected zone behind Alcatraz and the swirling eddy tucked behind the tip of Point Blunt, Angel Island. An accidental paucity of confetti makes the "Alcatraz Cone" appear larger than it is. Note also the divergence of currents into North Bay and South Bay.

protected water—and perhaps deliberately sail extra distance—before hazarding the countercurrents near the mark. They want to know now, and they want to know forty-five minutes from now on the next go-round. It is one of the magical, contrary, addictive attributes of yacht racing that the game is played on a shifting surface; and part of the necessary intelligence is stored only in the seat of the pants. To play the game well on the San Francisco Bay requires a grasp of certain principles, mental pictures of certain current flow, and judgments to be risked when the chips are down.

An all too frequent expectation is that the tide will turn first in the middle of the Bay. Instead, whether the tide is high or low, the first fingers of the new tide currents will form in a narrow ribbon along the San Francisco city front; later, similar thin bands of current will form along the Marin shore. These broaden and strengthen gradually until

(Text continued on page 52)

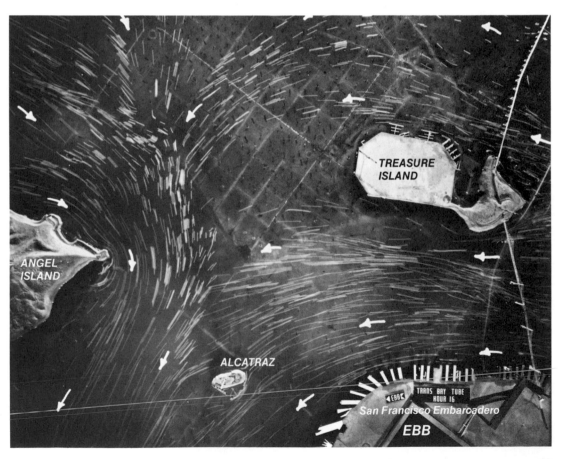

Ebb Tide

Ebb tide flow at the Bay Model. Model time is maximum ebb; net Delta outflow equals 16,000 cubic feet per second. In this Central Bay study, currents converge from northerly and southerly points before turning toward the Golden Gate. Tide-protected zones behind Alcatraz and Angel Island are smaller than they appear here.

The Adventures of the *Rubber Eagle*

Some folks are so nosy about West Bay waters that they will go out with nothing more in mind than contemplating the currents. One such venture took place on a clear day in a dry December. The vessel was the outboard-powered, inflatable *Rubber Eagle* According to her log, the current tables predicted a maximum ebb at 1:55 P.M., some five hours after a higher-high-water reading at the Golden Gate of +6.9 feet. A lower-low-water reading of –0.9 was predicted ninety minutes after maximum ebb. According to NOAA charts, ebb currents at 1:55 P.M. flowed toward the Golden Gate from all points inside the Bay: from Dumbarton Bridge, in the South Bay; from Carquinez Strait and Petaluma Creek, in the North; and from the marshiest reach of Richardson Bay in Marin. Ebb currents swept the entire San Francisco Bay estuary, flowing fastest through the deep channels and slowest in the shallows, and boiling into frothy confusion wherever land interfered. In the channel near Aquatic Park, the current ran 2 to 2.5 knots.

As the currents gathered and squeezed through the Golden Gate, their speed increased to 5.4 knots—all according to the NOAA's computer in Maryland. Just north of the Golden Gate, the shoals near Yellow Bluff were flecked with foam and pounded by the short, washtub waves of confused water (currents run strong here, and the bluffs deflect them toward the Gate). Under the bridge itself was a situation summed up neatly in the *Coast Pilot* : "Large current eddies near the foundation piers cause ships to veer off course."

The first goal of the *Rubber Eagle* was to steal a look at Alcatraz. Along the western face of The Rock, a small zone is sheltered from the outbound currents—but it is not so extensive as to offer much relief to a boat bound upcurrent. At any rate, it is unsafe to shave this western face too close. A bell buoy marks an area of submerged rocks; and between the buoy and the island, the situation is quite serious. Boats have ended their days here.

Musing upon the eerie solemnity possessed by Alcatraz even on a sunny day, the *Rubber Eagle* crew took a spin around to the eastern side, there to discover a sailboat caught in a very special trap. A faint westerly was blowing that day, and in the lee of the island this little cruiser was getting slim pickings. As it tried to sail toward San Francisco, it bumped a formidable tide rip. The water was prickly-topped and laden with debris. Beyond the rip, the ebb current flowed fast toward the Gate. On the island side was a large "bubble" of slow-moving water blocked by the island. Along the boundary between the two, the rip included water from the bubble that, in trying to join the ebb stream, was pushed back by the speed of the current. This deflected water formed a wall through which there could be no sailing—not without a heap more wind power than was available behind the island.

The way out of the trap, eventually, was to go the other way first. To sail south toward San Francisco, the cruiser had first to sail around the island to the north and west, being helped by the currents. Soon the sailors were back in the breeze and, though farther from their goal, were on their way at least, "crabbing" a bit (aiming upcurrent of where they really wanted to go) to compensate for the set of the current.

Pulled by the equivalent of eighteen powerful horses, the *Rubber Eagle* was far ahead of them on its own way to the city. At the Embarcadero, its crew espied ebb currents right up to the shoreline, even among the piers themselves. The currents flowed from the South Bay and wrapped around the base of Telegraph Hill, turning west. Friction with the piers and the somewhat shallower water close in slowed the currents. Speeds increased in the deeper water nearby, giving Blossom Rock Buoy the appearance of chugging up a white wake on its station one mile north of Coit Tower. There was no surface evidence of Blossom Rock itself, here at the crossroads of West Bay and South Bay traffic, though the rock had once protruded, making a good spot for seagulls and boatwrecks. Being indifferent to the one and downright aggravated by the other, progressive elements in the frontier port soon brought pressure to bear. In 1870, with a crowd to hurrah the fireworks, Blossom Rock was dynamited, blown right away to a depth of forty feet. The red-and-black buoy that exists now is hard as nails, but much softer than rock.

Farther west along the city front, the story was much the same: faster water in the channel, slower water close to shore; ebb currents throughout, even through the mooring buoys of the Liberty Ship *Jeremiah O'Brien* at Fort Mason and right to the wall at Gas House Cove. In this partly protected water between Fort Mason and the Marina breakwater, the current slowed noticeably in the last twenty feet before the wall. Small relief, that, if one is headed against the current.

The *Rubber Eagle* paused briefly to watch runners pass on their grassy way and a trawler yacht putter out from the Marina and into Gas House Cove for fuel; then she blasted out of that pocket with all eighteen horses breathing heavily and turned west to explore the outer face of the breakwater. Obvious ebb currents flowed past the starting-line buoys off the Golden Gate and St. Francis yacht clubs. Judging by the wake each buoy trailed in the current, there was slightly more flow past the outer St. Francis marker than the inner, just as theory says there should be.

Any difference between the water twenty feet off the beach and fifty feet off, however, was too subtle for the eyeball. A small patch of nearly slack water lay near the sand beach at the Marina Green. Lying roughly between the beach and the thin vertical post offshore—the "H-beam,"—it would have been useless in most sailing situations. The water inside the H-beam is off-limits to racing boats and is not a good place for nonracing boats. The sand bottom is covered about eight feet at mean lower low water, but the pipe that runs from the beach to the H-beam comes to within three feet of the surface.

Close by the H-beam but farther from the beach is Anita Rock, a major unseen landmark marked as a hazard by a twenty-foot tower and flashing light. Local racing rules usually keep keelboats to the north (outside) of Anita Rock. Because they are shallow, centerboarders are often not restricted.

Having heard one too many contradictory accounts of Anita Rock's particulars, the crew of the *Rubber Eagle* had requisitioned a whisker pole for use as a probe. With the motor off and the probe ready, the *Rubber Eagle* rode the ebb current toward the rock. The crew had no idea, actually, how much trouble they might or might not have finding the bottom. They were therefore prepared for anything—anything except the solid "thunk" of propellor against rock. "Aha!" they thought as one. "Anita Rock is quite shallow!"

Chastened and smarter, the captain conned his craft uptide again, shut her down, and put the motor on tilt. After that, the research was orderly. Anita proved also a big rock, extending some fifteen feet east of the tower, forty feet south, and twenty feet west. The time was low water, approximately; the height must therefore have been nine-tenths of a foot or less below mean lower low. Most of the depth readings were two feet or three feet. Weeds grew on the rock and grappled in the current with the whisker pole. The shallowest part lay about eight feet north, outside the tower, right where a boat cutting a tight corner would cross. That was where the motor had bumped. Then the rock quit, and the waters were deep again.

As the ebb cycle waned, there were subtle changes. At two hours, forty-five minutes past maximum ebb, currents had slowed perceptibly along the beaches to the west, at Presidio Shoal and Crissy Field. No back-currents existed in this area, even very close to the beach. Current flow was obvious, though it was less strong than the current in the channel nearby. Crissy Field Buoy, a white sphere three-tenths of a mile north of the Coast Guard station, is a popular racing mark. It is tethered on a shelf almost exactly where depths fall from thirty feet to seventy-five feet, and out in that deeper water there definitely was more current.

Having had a look at Crissy Field, almost in the shadow of the Golden Gate Bridge, the *Rubber Eagle* backtracked. Inside the H-beam the water was no longer slack; instead, it swirled east and north in a minor eddy. The yacht club buoys showed ebb, but an eddy had formed and was moving at about half a knot in front of where the end of breakwater juts into the Bay. This eddy extended not more than fifty yards along the breakwater or twenty yards from it and scarcely showed on the surface. Around the corner of the breakwater, near the rocks of Kite Flyers Central and the wall of Gas House Cove, a separate eddy had formed. It was thin and again offered nothing much in the way of relief, even to the racer.

In an ebb tide, with a westerly blowing, racing boats running downwind on cityfront courses hug the beach to minimize their exposure to the current. They are likely to take a dip into Gas House Cove in passing, but a dogleg all the way to the rocks would devour more value in distance traveled than a push from such a tiny eddy could make up—unless perhaps the winds are killing light, and all bets are off from the first. Because the piers of Fort Mason allow ebb currents to pass through, this cove at the Marina entrance is not well protected from the ebb (though the effective rock breakwater to the west makes it a very good place to duck a flood current).

The crew of the *Rubber Eagle* was aware of NOAA data indicating that flood tide begins ten minutes sooner along the Marina breakwater than at the Golden Gate, but they were unable to confirm this. Instead, some two hours after maximum ebb—with the slowing of the currents—the backcurrent in the cove also slowed; likewise the little eddy outside the lip of the breakwater. These were products of the strength of the ebb, and they dissipated with it. At 4:30 P.M.—about two and a half hours after maximum ebb—the yacht club buoys, Anita Rock, and Presidio Shoals all lay in currents still ebbing. As the currents eased, there was a sense of imminent change, a change that came from the west. Ever since maximum ebb, a large eddy of more than one knot had swirled in Baker Beach cove, west of the Golden Gate Bridge. That eddy now merged with the first finger of a genuine flood. In a narrow band, it sneaked around Fort Point close to the rocks; out in the middle of the Bay, the ebb continued at a knot or more. The *Rubber Eagle* took a quick look at the slight flood current now showing on Crissy Field Buoy, then zipped east to find a faint ebb yet at Anita Rock, slack water at the H-beam, and a faint ebb at the yacht club buoys along the breakwater. The eddy at the lip of the jetty had gone completely, though some backcurrent remained near the rocks inside the cove.

If tide books were perfect, the flood would have extended in a thin shoreline strip all the way from the Golden Gate to the Ferry Building, merging there with the ebb flowing from the North Bay into the South Bay (the "flebb") by 5:00 P.M. On this day, the development would take about half an hour longer. The light was failing and the evening growing uncomfortably cool in the damp socks of the ship's complement as they took one last blast west to find the flood now advanced, at 5:00, as far east as Presidio Shoals Buoy and moving at a fraction of a knot. The buoy trailed a marked wake, a reminder of how easy it is to overestimate current velocity by sight: the current could not have been more than three-tenths of a knot, but the wake trailed ten feet behind the buoy. Had the current been one knot, the wake would have formed a whirlpool behind the buoy with just a hint of white water—a condition that looks, intuitively, like three knots at least.

In the twilight, a smoke bomb signaled a boat in distress in the strait beyond the bridge. Engine failure most likely, or a dry gas tank (those two problems

Table 4 — CURRENT DIFFERENCES AND CONSTANTS

Station or Locality	Latitude ° ' North	Longitude ° ' West	Time difference h. m.	Velocity ratio
San Francisco Entrance				
(off Fort Pt.)	37 49	122 29	0.00	1.0
Golden Gate Br., ¾ mi. E. of	37 49	122 28	0.00	0.8
San Francisco Bay, South				
Alcatraz Island, ¼ mi. west of	37 50	122 26	−0.15	0.7
Alcatraz Island, south of	37 49	122 25	−0.25	0.5
Alcatraz Island, ¾ mi. east of	37 50	122 24	−1.00	0.5
Treasure Island ¾ mi. west of	37 49	122 24	−0.50	0.6
Treasure Island, ⅓ mi. east of	37 50	122 21	−0.40	0.5

	Latitude ° ' North	Longitude ° ' West	Beginning of Flood h. m.	Ebb h. m.
			Time meridian 120° W.	
St. F. Y. C. breakwater	37 48.5	122 26.5	−0.10	−1.50
Aquatic Park, 0.2 mi. west of	37 48.6	122 25.7	−0.35	−2.05
Pier 37	37 48.6	122 24.5	−1.35	−2.20
Pier 29	37 48.4	122 24.0	−1.10	−2.20
Pier 7	37 48.0	122 23.6	−0.55	−2.05
Pier 14	37 47.7	122 23.3	−0.55	−3.00
Pier 26	37 47.4	122 23.0	−1.40	−1.50
Pier 38	37 47.0	122 23.0	−0.25	−2.25
Pier 50	37 46.4	122 22.8	−1.40	−2.20
Bethlehem Pier No. 8	37 45.6	122 22.7	−1.20	−1.55
Pier 90, ½ mi. SE. of	37 44.5	122 22.4	−1.50	−2.05
Point Avisadero	37 43.7	122 21.3	−1.25	−0.40
" " ¾ mi. S. of	37 43.0	122 21.5	−1.30	−3.25

San Francisco Bay, South	Latitude ° ' North	Longitude ° ' West	Time difference h. m.	Velocity ratio
Oakland Outer Har. entrance	37 48	122 21	−1.10	0.5
Oakland Inner Har. entrance	37 48	122 20	−1.25	0.4
Oakland Harbor, Webster St.	37 48	122 16	−1.30	0.3
Rincon Point, ½ mi. east of	37 47	122 22	−0.20	0.7
Rincon Point, midbay	37 47	122 21	−0.50	0.7
Mission Rock, 0.6 mi. east of	37 46	122 22	−0.40	0.8
Mission Rock, 2 mi. east of	37 47	122 20	−1.05	0.6
Potrero Point, 2 mi. east of	37 45	122 20	−0.40	0.5
Point Avisadero, 1 mi. east of	37 44	122 20	−0.15	0.5
Sierra Point, 1.3 mi. ENE. of	37 41	122 22	−0.50	0.3
San Mateo Bridge	37 35	122 15	0.00	0.5
Dumbarton Pt., 2¼ mi. SE. of	37 28	122 04	+0.05	0.3

Station or Locality	Latitude ° ' North	Longitude ° ' West	Time difference h. m.	Velocity ratio
San Francisco Bay, North				
Yellow Bluff, ¾ mi. east of	37 50	122 27	−0.05	0.8
Alcatraz Island, ½ mi. N. of	37 50	122 25	+0.05	0.7
Pt. Blunt, Angel I., ¾ mi. SE. of	37 51	122 24	+0.20	0.3
Angel Island, ¾ mi. east of	37 52	122 24	+1.05	0.3
Richardson Bay entrance	37 51	122 28	−3.45	{0.3 {e0.1}
Raccoon Strait, off Pt. Stuart	37 52	122 27	−0.25	0.5
Raccoon Strait, off Hospital Cove	37 52	122 26	−0.40	0.5
Bluff Point, 0.1 mi. east of	37 53	122 26	−0.05	0.6
Southampton Shoal Light, ¼ mi. east of	37 53	122 24	+0.20	0.3
Point Richmond, 1½ mi. W. of	37 54	122 24	0.00	0.3
Red Rock, east of	37 56	122 26	+0.15	0.4
Pt. San Quentin, 1.9 mi. E. of	37 57	122 26	+0.40	0.5
San Pablo Bay				
Point San Pablo, midchannel	37 58	122 26	+0.50	0.6
Pinole Point, 1.2 mi. off	38 02	122 23	+1.20	0.5
Petaluma Creek entrance	38 07	122 30	+0.25	0.3
Carquinez Strait				
Mare Island Strait entrance, between dikes	38 04	122 15	+0.30	0.5
Mare Island Strait, off South Vallejo	38 05	122 15	+0.20	0.5
Crockett	38 04	122 13	+2.25	0.8
Benicia, south of	38 02	122 08	+2.30	0.6
Suisun Bay				
Roe Island, south of	38 04	122 02	+2.45	0.5
Chipps Island, south of	38 03	121 55	+3.40	0.7
Suisun Slough entrance	38 07	122 04	+1.30	0.4
Montezuma Slough, west entrance	38 08	122 03	+1.45	0.4
Bet. Roe Isl. and Ryer Isl.	38 04	122 01	+3.10	0.4
Montezuma Slough, east end, near bridge	38 05	121 53	+4.40	0.3
New York Slough, 0.6 mi. E. of Pt. Emmet	38 02	121 52	+3.55	0.4
Sacramento River				
Entrance (0.7 mi. SW of Chain I.)	38 03	121 52	+3.50	0.4
Pt. Sacramento, 0.3 mi. NE. of	38 04	121 50	+3.30	0.3
San Joaquin River				
Point Beenar, 0.8 mi. N. of	38 03	121 50	+4.50	0.4
Antioch Point, 0.3 mi. E. of	38 02	121 49	+4.30	0.4
West Island Lt. 0.5 mi. SE. of	38 01	121 46	+4.30	0.2
Vulcan Island, ½ mi. E. of	37 59	121 23	+5.50	0.2

account for most of the Coast Guard rescues on the West Bay, and the Coasties do a lot of business at sundown). The smoke floated in on the light breeze and did not dissipate until it was nearly to Alcatraz. By then a rescue boat dispatched from the station at Crissy Field had reached the scene, its green light flashing, and was doing whatever there was to be done.

The captain of the *Rubber Eagle* made one last, fast swing around the yacht club buoys, saw that the flood had not yet arrived, and took off across the still-ebbing midbay currents toward home port in Belvedere. On the way, he checked in at Yellow Bluff, where a thin band of flood current crept in along the rocks.

Gunning for home in earnest, he passed east across the mouth of Richardson Bay, with its slack current, and found the least mite of ebb remaining on the black buoy at the tip of Belvedere (Peninsula Point), then lost himself in reveries of Irish Coffee. He knew the ebb would continue awhile in the middle; but outside the Golden Gate, flood currents were converging and forcing their way through the strait. Inside they were fanning out and soon would take over the channels, blocking the ebb completely. In another few hours the flood would turn even the river flow in Carquinez Strait, and there would be no ebb currents anywhere in the San Francisco Bay estuary.

they take over the entire Bay. The West Bay is center ring in our local circus, and the city front has the bleachers. Together they deserve a close look.

The events witnessed by the *Rubber Eagle* in the West Bay have their counterparts elsewhere and at other times. In shallow areas the current will be slowed. Any inlet along the shore or any obstruction jutting into the flow will cause some disruption of the current: in an inlet, the current will slow and perhaps eddy; behind major obstructions will be areas of protected water offering relief from the current and perhaps an eddying flow. Rips may form between the main current and an eddying pocket of water.

Tide rips may also form wherever powerful currents run side by side in opposing directions as they often do during transition periods. The sea water, blue and dark, floods alongside the lighter green or brownish ebb, and between them licks pandemonium laden with any debris that floats. Even between currents not powerful enough to form an angry rip, there will be a line of demarcation—one of the *tide lines* for which San Francisco Bay sailors are forever watching. A tide line can be a subtle thing, showing no more evidence than a different texture on the water's sur-

face. When neither wind nor currents are strong, a long, meandering line between flood and ebb may appear as a narrow, smooth band that reflects light differently. As a further sign, even a mild breeze will form recognizably different patterns on the surfaces of flood and ebb. In a westerly, flood currents are going the same direction as the wind. The effect is to smooth the wave pattern. Ebb currents are going against the wind. The effect is to make the surface choppier, with the waves close together and steep. A tide line may also appear between two streams of water going the same direction at different speeds.

The change from flood to ebb has only a few features different from the ebb–flood transition. Flood currents prevail until three hours after maximum flow. At that time, water ebbs from the South Bay and flows into the North Bay—the reverse of the "flebb" tide observed at three hours after maximum ebb. Throughout the flood-tide cycle there exist pockets of protected water from the Marina to the Embarcadero. Cityfront racing fleets then hug the shore on the upwind leg, a grueling procedure known as "short-tacking the city front." They do so at their peril, passing the popular fishing spots at Aquatic Park and Fort Mason, where fisherfolk find it well worth the occasional loss of line and lead for the pleasure of planting one on a yachtie's head.

Late in the flood cycle, countercurrents grow in these pockets. These eddies are much more useful to the racing skipper than the little bit of relief afforded shoreside during the ebb. A racing boat tacking west past Fort Mason will take a tack into the cove below the Marina breakwater and may find itself suddenly being propelled the way it wants to go, rather than being pushed back. About ninety minutes after maximum flood, these narrow bands of countercurrent begin to peep out from behind their barriers. They join forces, and by two hours after maximum flood become a steady ribbon of ebb running from Aquatic Park west past Fort Mason, the Marina, and Crissy Field to the Golden Gate, where they join a Baker Beach eddy that has been active since maximum flood.

A similar process takes place, somewhat later, along the northern shore. A long arm of ebbing current will be seen arcing across the mouth of Richardson Bay, sweeping past Yellow Bluff, and out the Gate along the rocks at Lime Point while a weakened flood continues in the middle. The waters between Alcatraz and Sausalito tend to slacken briefly at the transition, then turn to ebb until, by three hours after maximum current, there is no flood remaining on the West Bay.

Only very high river stages alter the currents noticeably in the San Francisco Bay. NOAA's tidal predictions account for average seasonal variations in river discharge, so it takes exceptional circumstances to fool them. U.S. Geological Survey findings indicate that river discharge may vary from a one-percent component of ebb tide flow at low river stages to ten percent at high river stages. There is negligible difference in the current activity of the Bay whether the discharge rate is a dry summer's five thousand cubic feet per second or a wet winter's twenty thousand. An unusually heavy spring runoff might reach seventy thousand cubic feet per second, in which North Bay currents will begin to ebb, muddy and brown, as soon as the flood weakens, and the ebb in the middle of the Bay will flow stronger than predicted.

Tides and currents are studied in detail at the Army Corps of Engineers' Bay Model in Sausalito. This huge facility offers a facsimile of the entire Bay and Delta, with the depths shown on exaggerated scale. The model is run, with tides pumped in and out, only when studies are under way; by calling ahead, however, it is possible to find out the hours of operation. A great deal can be learned from watching a tidal cycle that takes minutes instead of hours and happens all within view. It is just like real life: the tide comes in, the tide goes out, and the currents run every which way.

A big sky and a classic yacht: Yucca beats toward Yellow Bluff.

IV: WEATHER IN NORTHERN CALIFORNIA

FOR MANY A SAILOR from Los Angeles and other south-of-Market climes, a trip to the San Francisco Bay is something of a pilgrimage. Wind, reliable wind, is the theme, and all summer long the Bay delivers. There is scarcely another spot on the globe where one could schedule a Heavy Weather Slalom for the July 4 weekend and trust it to bluster, just like clockwork. In summer, the region generates its own powerhouse weather. In winter, the local scene alternates calm with whatever weather system may be passing, west to east, from the Pacific.

Winter

Our most variable season is winter—not the calendar winter, but the months from November through February. The *Coast Pilot* for the Pacific Coast reports that calms occur in winter 15 to 40 percent of the time inside the Bay and 10 to 12 percent of the time on the ocean. It is a time of quiet. Except when storms are passing through, the winds are gentle, and sailors like to joke that winter is the true warm season. Even in cool temperatures, ghosting along on a hint of a northerly with the decks dry in bright sunshine can be balm, honest balm, compared to the wind chill of a spray-faced, fogbound sail in July.

While an early storm might sneak in from the south, bringing rain and thunder whipped up off the coast of Mexico, the meat-and-potatoes storms of the California rainy season wait for business far to the west and northwest: three-fourths of the region's precipitation falls between December and March. In winter, the Pacific High Pressure Zone takes a position well south of our 37-degree, 48-minute latitude, thus clearing the storm track to the California coast. The storms that strike the Bay Area are the same storms that sweep eastward, taking rain and snow inland. Meteorologists call them *extra-tropical cyclones*. They form far out over the ocean, where a cold air mass from the polar region may rush southward alongside a mass of moist, warm tropical air bound north. Friction eventually disturbs some region along their unstable boundary, and cold air begins to press under the warm air. At the same time, warm air will rise over the cold; and where that warm air rises, barometric pressure drops. Meteorologists note this zone of decreased pressure on their weather maps as a *low*.

Where cold air displaces warm, we speak of a cold front. Where warm air displaces cold, we speak of a warm front. At maturity, an extra-tropical cyclone consists of a cold front linked to a warm front, with winds rotating counter-clockwise around the low and the entire system moving either east or north-of-east at a likely speed of seven hundred miles per day.

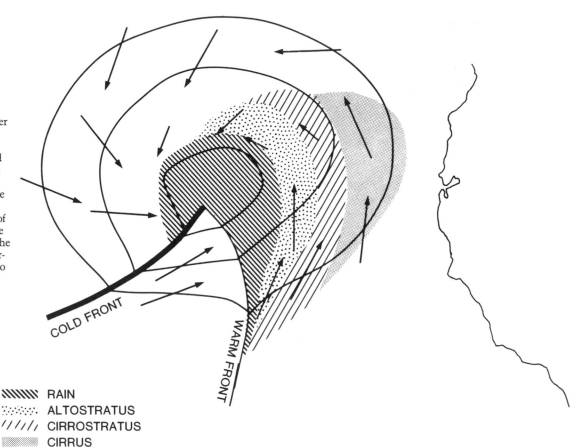

Figure 5. The extra-tropical cyclone, more familiar to Bay Area residents as a typical winter storm. In this case, the low-pressure zone surrounding the juncture of warm front and cold front will pass directly over San Francisco Bay. Southerly winds and high cirrus clouds announce the arriving storm. The clouds lower, bringing rain just ahead of the frontal system and along the cold front—the *squall line*. As the storm passes, west to east, clearing skies will bring windshifts to the west and north.

COLD FRONT

WARM FRONT

≈≈≈≈ RAIN
:::::: ALTOSTRATUS
///// CIRROSTRATUS
▓▓▓▓ CIRRUS

In figure 5 we see the sketch of a storm. Where the moist, warm air rises, rain forms as a function of the altitude: in rising, the air cools by expansion. Cool air cannot hold as much moisture as warm air, and when temperatures fall below the dew point, water vapor condenses to form clouds and rain.

Wispy high ice clouds—called *cirrus*—typically precede the low by five hundred miles, or a little less than a day's traveling time for the storm. Barometers begin falling about the time cirrus appear in the sky (except in the frequent case that the cirrus come from a dissipating storm or from a sys-

tem passing too far north). Some three hundred miles ahead of the low, cloud formations lower and thicken into *altostratus* at eight thousand to twenty thousand feet; these translucent sheets often show dark bands at the lower elevations. Behind the altostratus come the puffy *cumulus*, flat-bottomed *stratocumulus*, and the *nimbostratus*—reaching almost to the ground and bringing rain. Variations of the Latin *nimbus* are applied to any cloud that produces rain (there are those who swear they have sailed in a nimbofog). A good weather eye can deduce much from cloud formations, but the conditions that produce one storm will often toss off several storms close together; and when that happens, the sky may fill with a mixture of cloud types that defy ready interpretation.

West Coast yachters lean toward the lackadaisical when it comes to watching the sky. Elsewhere in the world, weather fronts threaten year-round, and amateur meteorology is taken for granted among the basic skills. Bay sailors who go traveling, whether racing or cruising, will do well to bone up. Locally, however, weather fronts are common only a few months per annum—emphatically unpopular months for ocean cruising and not the peak months for Bay sailing—and cloud study is blissfully ignored by many who get along quite well, thank you. Yet those who sail through the winter can hardly ignore that even more direct indicator of coming weather, the abrupt and auspicious change in wind direction.

The strongest winds of winter often arrive from the southwest or southeast, announcing the advent of a frontal system. As the system passes, winds shift to the north or west, again with considerable velocity. The cause is clear if we consider again the counterclockwise flow of winds in the extra-tropical cyclone, as shown in figure 5. A storm passing directly overhead would first deliver winds from a generally southerly direction, along the eastern edge of the storm. Rains and rising temperatures come later (at the arrival of the warm front), followed by a period of clearing skies and southwesterly winds. Then comes the cold front, pushing before it a nimbostratus wall of cloud, with rain; and later comes a windshift to the west or north. **As a rule of thumb for frontal systems, winds from southerly directions advertise an incoming storm; winds from westerly or northerly directions bespeak its departure.**

Many of our winter storms reach the coastline at an advanced "age." Late in the life of an extra-tropical cyclone, the cold front may catch up with the warm front, lifting the warm air mass entirely away from the earth's surface. This condition is called an *occluded front*. The warm front is blocked, or occluded, from reaching the ground. A similar cycle of windshifts will occur, but the rain will come all at once, as the single front passes through, and without a distinct period of clearing. Winter storms tend to approach from the west, the north, or the quadrant between. The farther north, the colder the air and the better the news for frozen-water sport in the Sierra. The farther south the origin of the storm, the warmer the entire system and the more likely it is to bring rain and slush to high elevations—and more tolerable wet sailing on the Bay.

The first strong winds of winter never fail to catch a few residents of the anchorages *in derelictus*, and the cause is not always a storm. Less frequently, but often enough to be part of the winter weather picture, powerful northerlies sweep the interior valley and the Bay Area. This happens whenever the great currents of polar continental air "skip their banks." Pressed outward from northern latitudes in the frigid, high-pressure interiors of the continent, these dry, cold currents usually follow paths east of the Sierra Nevada, chilling the deserts of Nevada and the plains of the Midwest. When polar air interlopes along the coast, it brings a bitter whitecap wind that sings off key in the rigging. And it sings loud, which makes for a hectic time in the anchorages. Radar watchers at Vessel Traffic Service keep a close check on the positions of anchored ships in the South Bay. Elsewhere, poorly tethered boats break loose from their moorings or drag anchor, presenting danger to themselves and innocent bystanders. Occasionally the Coast Guard is drawn into the act of rescuing these boats. At other times the owners of neighboring craft are to be seen rowing through the choppy waters, playing good Samaritan to a mess caused by sloppy anchoring techniques and inattention to lines and chafe points.

The Sausalito anchorage has troubles with both northern and southern exposure. Around the corner in Belvedere Cove, the south is the only unsheltered direction, but there is enough open water to fetch formidable waves in a southerly. Wise skippers check their tether and perhaps take extra precautions when storms approach. While several harbors around the Bay have some sort of exposure, these are the only two areas where significant numbers of boats ride to moorings outside a breakwater.

Calm weather has its own hazards, especially when temperatures are cold. While we think of summer as the foggy season along the coast, winter is the time for fog formed inland, which sometimes intrudes on the coast. "Ground fog" is what most parts of the country call the *radiation fog* so common in the Sacramento River Delta in winter; because the low-lying wetlands are especially prone to this condition, it becomes "tule fog" in our local lingo. (Tules are the plants, much like bulrushes, that abound in the Delta shallows.)

On clear, cold nights, the ground and the marshes radiate heat readily to the outer atmosphere. If winds are calm, say zero to five knots, the ground becomes colder than the air above. That relatively warm air then radiates its own heat to the ground, losing even more heat wherever it touches the ground. With the cooling of the air comes condensation and radiation fog. In a near-perfect calm, such a tule fog may float shin high, like the dry-ice fog in a Busby Berkeley musical. A mild breeze circulates the fog as it forms, carrying it higher, though too much wind will halt the process. During a particularly long spell of quiet, cold weather, the entire northern valley may get into the act of radiating fog, even to depths of several hundred feet.

Just as water is forever seeking its own level, air seeks always to equalize its pressure. It flows from a cold area to a warm area. The Bay in winter stays warmer than the valley, thanks to the tempering effect of the ocean, which loses less heat than the land. The result in such times is a land breeze, moving toward the ocean and bearing tule fog through Carquinez Strait and the gaps in the Berkeley Hills. Over the Bay it may be reinforced by fog radiated from the Bay's own marshland. Such tule fogs are capable of reducing visibility to dangerous minimums on the rivers, the Bay, and the approaches; these fogs are far more likely to close the airports than any mere rainstorm.

Calm weather is a familiar fact of winter, and so is the tule fog. While winter rouses the fiercest wind velocities of the year—storm winds reaching fifty and seventy-five knots on the ocean—the long calms between bring the average wind strength to the lowest levels of the year. November through January, average wind speeds as recorded in the Pacific Coast *Pilot* run from eight to eight and a half knots. In February the figure climbs, and the numbers continue to increase throughout the spring while major changes take place in the atmosphere. The Bay really has only two seasons, winter and summer. Between come transition periods distinct enough to be called spring or autumn.

Summer

The first signs of summer come about March. Earth's tilt on its axis and its orbit around the sun produce what our near-sighted way of thinking calls "the northward migration of the sun." And as the sun's overhead position edges north, the northern latitudes grow warmer. Temperatures rise in California's inland valley just as surely as temperatures rise in mid-Pacific. The stage is set for the marriage of these warming trends to create, ironically, Mark Twain's "coldest winter of my life one summer in San Francisco."

As the season warms, the Pacific High Pressure Zone moves north to latitudes west of San Francisco; that event in itself is enough to alter our weather. It is time to look closely at the Pacific High. Even in its winter position south of 37 degrees, 48 minutes (the Golden Gate), the high has blocked many storms from the western coast of the continent. Most storms that reach North America are centered north of the San Francisco Bay for this reason. As the high draws north in the summer, it becomes an even more effective blockade, enforcing California's dry climate and rerout-

Bohemia's *spinnaker pole rolls discomfitingly close to the water. Her genoa is wrapped around the headstay, and even though the mainsail and boom are held out of sight to weather by a preventer strap—so far—the crew may at any moment be refreshed (crash course) on the old question, "Why is a boom called a boom?"*

ing storms to the north, begetting the wet climates of Oregon and Washington.

Growing stronger in the spring as solar energy strikes the Northern Hemisphere more directly, the Pacific High tends to center somewhere between San Francisco and Hawaii, about a thousand miles west of the Gate. There it weighs heavily on the surface of the sea. This weight is born of an influx of air from the tropics: superheated in the equatorial regions, it rises and flows northward. As it travels, much of the air cools and descends; the downward press of this tall, widespread mound of air builds the pressure of the Pacific High Pressure Zone.

Since air acts to equalize its pressure, winds flow inward from all directions toward a low, and outward from a high. Unlike a low-pressure system, which in the northern hemisphere forms counterclockwise wind flows, the high forms a clockwise flow that dominates the broad weather of the Pacific. The southern reach forms the *trade winds* blowing toward Hawaii; no less usefully to the traders of yore or the sailors of today, winds on the northern reach blow toward the continent. On the eastern reach, winds blow north to south; these become the prevailing northwesterlies of the California coast.

Much of the behavior of the Pacific High is predictable. Rather than take a beeline (rhumb line) course to the islands, Hawaii-bound sailing craft from California customarily make some distance south, then turn more to a westerly heading. This dogleg takes them into the trades. Returning from Hawaii, the best track often lies to the north, to catch the winds headed toward the coast across the "top" of the high. In the high itself there is very little wind, and it comes fitfully, with calms.

But the high has more moods than can be accounted for by squiggles on a chart. Sometimes in midsummer it will break into several parts, or take a position farther south than expected, with a confounding effect upon sailing routes. This was the case in the "Turtle Transpac" of 1979, when eighty-one boats enroute from Los Angeles to Honolulu split into two groups: those who found the wind by sailing much farther south than usual, and those whom experience led to latitudes where the textbook promised wind—where instead there was only the muggy frustration of the high. For the latter, there were days of calm so thorough the sea mirrored the colors in the cloud. Or the wind came in wisps day after day; it was like sailing Lake Merritt: fickle and endless.

This was a strange turn of events, even more so when similar oceanic weather a year later tricked and teased (and in some cases rewarded) entries in two races from San Francisco to Kauai: a solo race sponsored by the Singlehanded Sailing Society, and a fully-crewed race sponsored by Ballena Bay Yacht Club. However strange, the events clearly lay within the statistical range. We can moan about it, like all weather, but there is not much more to do except outflank it, given whatever is our draw of smarts and luck.

In the transition from winter to summer weather, March and April are unstable months off the coast of Northern California. In the Gulf of the Farallones, spring storms are rare; but stiff stuff—in the 17- to 28-knot range—will blow as much as 40 percent of the time. The interior valley meanwhile grows hotter while the Pacific High circulation grows stronger. The countryside languishes in a mild haze, the air drawing moisture from the hills thick and green with grass from winter rains. It is a time of waiting.

The wait is not long. Northwesterly winds ride the ocean approaches, pushed by the High Pressure Zone and blocked from the continent by the coastal mountains. In the valley, at Stockton and French Camp and Whiskey Slough, the overheated air moves up and away. Weather maps soon show the valley as a region of low atmospheric pressure. This low is different from the low at the center of a storm: here, no conflicting polar and tropical air masses whirl about each other; instead there is only the spiraling uplift of overheated air in its search to equalize air pressure. At sea

Norma Jean, *walking a thin line of control, depowers the mainsail as Etchells-class sloops approach a leeward mark.*

Doing the foredeck stretch. Lois Lane's tactician, standing in the background, is dressed as though he stepped aboard directly from sailing a 505 dinghy—and he did.

the air is cold and dense. Air pressure is high. Between sea and valley is one—count it, one—sea-level opening: the Golden Gate. And the wind comes busting through.

It is this onshore pressure gradient that fuels the summer westerly of San Francisco Bay, which dominates the sailing from March through October. Sea breeze is a conventional weather pattern for any temperate coastline, but this is a sea breeze of heroic proportions, so prevalent that nighttime land breezes—also conventional in most corners of the world—come as oddments here. Only the far southern shores of the South Bay develop a land breeze (blowing from the land) often enough to merit mention in the *Coast Pilot*, "and even here it is an infrequent occurrence." Statistically, the nighttime breeze over the Bay tends to remain westerly (though nighttime sailors will find many local quirks). Morning breezes will be light. They may come from anywhere—or not at all: a flat calm. The cry of a gull carries far over quiet water. A rowing shell may treat the early morning Bay as a pond, cutting swiftly across a surface mirror-smooth and blinding in the eastern light.

At some time in a quiet morn, the waters in the Golden Gate will darken with a first breath of wind. Eyes already watching the west will spot the darkening ruffles in the strait and recognize, "The wind is coming." The westerly may hang in the strait temporarily, but eventually it will move. It will move quickly or slowly, but either way gives alert crews time to prepare. The sudden heeling of boats farther west and the darkening of the water are the visible signs of an approaching wall of wind. Watching the westerly come, crews in T-shirts and shorts reach for sweaters and foul-weather gear, knowing it is possible in two minutes to go from sail-slatting idleness to rail-down speed and spray.

The sudden boom of the westerly into a calm bay is a memorable and frequent event. Statistically, however, the westerly runs all day. In the summertime, winds between eleven o'clock at night and nine o'clock in the morning flow from the west at three to ten knots, increasing to between six and fifteen knots late in the morning, and growing to between fourteen and twenty knots in the afternoon. In the evening, the westerly tends to subside. But this is only the daily cycle, and these are average figures. Cycles in the strength of the westerly also take place over a week or so. At its height, the sea breeze may be blowing ten knots at dawn and more than thirty in the afternoon. In the days following, intensities will lower, then build again. These longer cycles are bound up with yet another cyclical phenomenon, the summer fog.

Fog is equivalent to cloud, a stratus cloud of water vapor condensed into a mass of microscopic water droplets suspended in air. Ocean temperatures colder than the air above provoke a summer fog unlike the radiation fog of winter. When the fog gods smile on us in summer, they present *advection fog*. Advection refers to the horizontal movement of air; this creates fog mostly in the daytime. While some summers in San Francisco run relatively gray and others relatively clear, so prevalent is the advection fog of the West Coast that the *Coast Pilot* speaks of a semipermanent fog bank that may be a hundred miles wide, sometimes retreating from the coast, sometimes holding near. In its development we see the influence of the Pacific High and the clockwise motion of air in the North Pacific, which builds currents of water beneath the currents of air.

The Northern California coast does not run directly north and south. Rather, it runs about southeast. The prevailing winds approximate that course, sometimes blowing directly down the coast, more often slightly toward the coast. These are the northwesterlies, and they literally push the surface waters along. But these movements of wind and water alike are affected by the rotation of the earth and its product, the Coriolus force. There are no straight lines of trajectory in the Pacific. The southeasterly flow that we call the California Current is bent to the right (toward the west), as are all trajectories in the northern hemisphere. This curl draws the surface currents away from the coast. One could say that the earth, as it rotates to the east, leaves the current behind. Cold waters rise from the depths to take their place, and temperatures drop 10 to 15 degrees lower than in mid-Pacific.

Before they reach the coast, the warm winds from the Pacific must cross this region of chilly water. Because these winds have come across thousands of miles of open ocean, they are saturated with water vapor. Swiftly cooled by the coastal current, their vapor condenses into the coastal fog bank, and six major gaps in the coastal range—primarily the Golden Gate—become the air-conditioning shafts of a hard-driving natural ventilation system.

This fog bank typically reaches elevations of five hundred to fifteen hundred feet, where it is held back by an *inversion layer* of hot, dry air subsiding from the eastern zone of the high. (We speak of an inversion wherever a layer of warm air rides above a layer of cooler air.) It is this inversion that blesses the peak of Mount Tamalpais with sunshine even while ocean and Bay are blotted out, and horns blare in the mist.

When the wind funnel and the condensation elements are operating full blast, the fog may penetrate at night even into the central valley. The wind may blow day and night, and near the ocean, only the most protected pockets see the sun. Then this incursion gradually causes its own demise: so thoroughly does the wind cool the valley that the inland air is no longer hot enough to keep the fog machine working. The fog retreats. Afternoon westerlies in the Bay abate and may disappear entirely at night. Golden Gate Park fills with the skimpily clad and the Golden Gate fills with sailors saying, "Oh yeah, this is nice."

Such conditions will last a day or more, but the valley is heating again all this while. Air pressure in the valley lowers, and the cycle resumes. A tiny beret of fog will soon cock itself on the headland above the bridge. The next day will bring more fog, and it will show earlier. The fog and wind increase until the blast is strong enough to lower val-

ley temperatures. Then winds will ease again. Thus the oft-heard half-truth, "San Francisco Bay doesn't blow, the valley sucks." The other half of that truth is that the incoming breeze is propelled by the press of winds from the Pacific High—an important variable. If the high is weak and circulation slow, wind and fog may "level out"—never cooling the valley enough to peak and decline, and maintaining a stratus layer over the Bay and approaches for days on end—until the high regains its punch.

A number of local influences act on winds within the Bay region. In the North Bay, winds south of west are part of a picture formed by the channeling of the hills and the heating of the Petaluma and Napa Valleys. During periods of extreme heat, these valleys to the north occasionally act as miniature high-pressure systems, forcing air out and creating a northerly flow through the North Bay. Usually, this flow will break up somewhere between Angel Island and Richmond, leaving a strip of calm between itself and the westerly that continues through the Gate. This phenomenon is most often seen in September or October. Local geography may also create southeasterly winds, as happens at Hamilton Air Force Base in Marin County. It is all part of the microclimate system of the region: areas exposed to the fog receive cool, moist summers while protected areas a mere crow-hop away bask in dry, hot summers.

A complete wind-and-fog cycle typically takes a week or so. It might run half that long, or twice that long, but anyone who pays attention can make some good guesses about the next day's weather. August is the foggiest month: fog signals operate 40 to 50 percent of the time in the ocean approaches and 15 to 20 percent of the time in the Golden Gate. The disposition of the fog inside the Bay depends on the power of the wind behind it and the quirks of local geography. A fog close to the water surface may pour through the Golden Gate in a long stream straight toward the Berkeley Hills, leaving all to the north and south in sunshine. A slight southerly shift in the wind might bring fog to Rich-

Fog, Finn, and a light touch on the tiller extension.

Airing out the bottom—and waiting for the rudder to get a bite. A T's J crewman turns an accusing eye.

ardson Bay and Raccoon Strait, which usually are clear.

The state of the tide will affect fog. Ebb tide currents tend to be warmer than ocean water. On reaching this warmer water, incoming fog may break up and turn patchy. A more dramatic tidal influence is sometimes seen on a clear, bright day when the tide turns to flood. As it enters the Bay, the cool water from the Gulf of the Farallones may bring with it a thick blanket, swift and sudden and right at surface level, causing *whiteout* through the whole of the West Bay. The navigator's ears will then be cocked for the low moans of horns at Alcatraz and Lime Point, or the telltale howl of the Porsches in Sausalito.

Whiteout follows when fog forms right at surface level. On most of our foggy days, however, fog forms well above the surface, leaving ample visibility on the water. The fog deck may ride anywhere from fifty to fifteen hundred feet off the surface. Tourists shiver on Nob Hill and predict rain. Locals shrug it off as high fog. It is the Bay, right in character. As Harold Gilliam points out in his thorough *Weather of the San Francisco Bay Region*, fog depends only on the cooling of air below its dew point, not on contact with cool water. The daily invasion from the west creates a special, cool climate over the Bay capable of taking over the job. Beneath the warm air aloft, a layer of cool air settles in, with temperatures dropping toward the fifties—toward the temperature of the water. There being no appreciable difference between water and air temperatures, the air at lower elevations is clear. But this lower-level air is cool enough to stimulate stratus where it contacts the warm air above. The outcome is high fog, a fog that is wetter the farther out to sea it has formed, dryer the closer to shore.

Thanks to the continual press of the sea breeze, this cool lower level of air takes root over the Bay and pretty much holds its own throughout the summer. Its depth will vary along with other elements of the wind-and-fog cycle; sometimes it drops low enough to blot out the roof of the Lime Point Lighthouse, with stratus formed above it, enveloping

the bridge. At the height of the cycle, cool air may push the inversion layer upwards of fifteen hundred feet. The fog deck then will ride even above the hills. Visibility on the water is fine, but the city and suburbs will be shaded in the coldest and gloomiest weather the fog season has to offer. The most true-blooded of San Franciscans, who dote on their fog, can be set to grumbling if this extremely high fog persists too long. The fog deck's height is affected also by the passage of high-pressure ridges and low-pressure troughs. These weak, upper-level disturbances usually have no effect upon Bay Area weather beyond holding fog low—beneath a ridge of high pressure—or drawing it high into the hills—below a trough of low pressure.

The regularity of the summer westerly maintains the lower layer of cool air and the high fog associated with it. Early spring and late fall lack this regularity; they are thus the seasons that run the greatest risk of surface-level fog and whiteout. Regardless of season, surface-level fog is also likely to ensue at the end of a heat wave. Every summer, and with greater frequency in the autumn months, the old reliable westerly shuts down for an interval or several intervals. A high-pressure cell moving into the coast—perhaps a renegade spur of the Pacific High—will do the job neatly. Air pressures equalize over land and sea. Flags hang limp, and temperatures soar as the high-pressure system clamps down. With the ventilation turned off, automobile exhausts and factory fumes turn the sky dirty brown, and those who can, make fast tracks to the beaches. These "inversions" typically last two or three days, but one mean heat wave in 1971 persisted five days, sending the thermometer to 105 degrees in the city and poisoning the air to obnoxiously noxious intensities. In such extremes, heat and the weight of traffic may sag the Bay Bridge as much as ten feet from its normal 220-foot midspan height.

A mild heat wave is a pleasant thing. San Francisco Bay sailors do not lack for wind, and they are only too delighted with a few days of the sort of shirts-off weather enjoyed in

the Catalina Channel. But when the wind goes away completely and for too long a time, some measure of comfort lies in knowing that, when at last the pressure imbalance is restored between valley and sea, the westerly will return with authority. Winds may jump from zero to twenty-five knots seemingly on the instant. Not even the arrival of a winter storm is more forceful than the summer westerly reclaiming its own.

A general increase of air pressure over the region—and with it a moderating of the sea breeze—is characteristic of October and November weather. As the sun's overhead position drops south, the Pacific High weakens and also moves south. The valley cools. Ocean temperatures have been raised by summer heat. And even though the Northern Hemisphere as a whole is cooling toward winter, these factors combine in a subsiding of the onshore pressure gradient. Indian Summer casts its spell. Autumn brings the mildest and smoggiest weather of the year to the waters of the Bay, along with intervals of dry, hot northeasterlies driven outward from high-pressure cells situated over the Northwest. Anything is likely then, from placid zephyrs to the violent "fire winds" that keep the Forest Service on tenterhooks and inspire rangers to post "Fire Danger 100%" warnings at park entrances.

If it is possible to say that occasional abnormalities are normal, then we may count these infrequent northeasterlies as part of San Francisco Bay's normal weather pattern. And we may add the summer rain. But how quickly we forget: rarely a summer passes without at least one rainfall, but no sooner will the skies open than perplexed groups gather on the docks at Port Sonoma and around the wharves of China Basin agreeing, "I never saw anything like *this* before!"

Few storms skip through the blockade of the Pacific High Pressure Zone in the summer, but there are rains that come from other quarters. Occasionally a storm will steal away from its rightful stomping grounds in the Gulf of Mexico, gallop across the continent, and strike the Sierra. Even more occasionally, such a storm will clear the Sierra and make its way to the Bay. The house bet then calls for light sprinkles.

But there are other bets. When San Francisco has one of its rare thunderstorms, complete and replete with heavy rainfall and bold lightning displays, the Gulf of Mexico is probably the source. Long before the head-shaking and the tongue-clucking are done, however, this maverick will be on its way out. The westerly will be marshaling its forces, soon to return with vigor. Gardeners go back to sprinkling, and the head-shakers and tongue-cluckers go back to forgetfulness for another year. Such are the lessons of the San Francisco Bay.

How many boatlengths to the line? The helmsman of Whistle Wing V *will time his Big Boat Series start by the point man's hand signals.*

Built in Tiburon in 1885, the sloop Freda *has known loving hands.*

V: SAN FRANCISCO'S OCEAN

"It's the wilderness experience that brought me into sailing. It's more of an escape route, or dynamic, than anything else I've found."
—ALEXIS MONSON

"40 on the stupid!"
—SARAH B.

*S*ET OUT ONE CLEAR eve for a sail west, with a westerly breeze to stir the sails and the downtown towers flashing gold astern. Let the gentlest of chop lick the leeward rail. Let a quick tug on the leech cord take the flutter out of the jib. Ahead, the day's fishing boats cut fast wakes inbound through the Golden Gate. The headlands darken into silhouette against the sun's decline. If it is a normal evening in Northern California, it is time already to pull out the long underwear and the extra socks as Fort Point passes the port beam and the bridge passes overhead. For a moment, the rustling of water blends with the growl of commuter traffic, homebound to redwood canyons where Mercedes Benz are common as dirt—and much cheaper.

On the north wall of the strait, scarfaced Franciscan sandstone lifts into hills one thousand feet higher than the water. It plunges 382 feet to thick silt, beyond sight in the depths below, and then down through the silt to the carved bedrock that once was a mountain pass and a stream bed. The strait is narrow, a gate to a broader world. Off the quarter, the sun's slanting light bends rainbows in the spray. Off the bow lies no sharp horizon; instead, the watery air—interchanging moisture between water and air—merges the two. The sun grows large and sinks all at once, stealing gold

dust from the sea, glow escaping up the cheeks of the hills.

Beyond the Gate the ocean opens wide. Beyond the wind funnel the winds ease. The hull lifts to the swell on a view from Point Reyes to Point San Pedro. Lights flicker among the hills, lighthouses switch on, and the channel buoys begin flashing, glimmering across a sea turned mercury-calm in the twilight. A tanker grumbles west, bound to sea. A container ship grumbles east toward the strait. When the stars come out, they *really* come out. The night deepens to compelling clarity.

This is the peace of the sea, and the purposefulness in simply being, that lies at the center of Alexis Monson's not-so-accidentally contradictory "escape route, or dynamic." All who love the sea have felt it. When it is good, there is nothing better. Those who love the sea beyond infatuation feel it all the more for knowing also the other moods of the sea: the days of too much weather, of slabsided, bonechilling waves and bumps and bruises and the thought, "Yessir, if Sarah B. could see me now, she'd bet the whole 40 on me!"

The coastal bight that is our front yard, the Gulf of the Farallones, reaches south thirty-four miles from Point Reyes to Point San Pedro, and westward some twenty-three miles to the Farallon Islands. Nowhere in the Gulf of the

71

Farallones is the water as deep as in the Golden Gate, where fast currents keep themselves a path. A long, shallow sandbar arcs around the Gate's approach, a semicircle extending halfway to the San Francisco Approach Buoy, prevented from damming the approach only by the scouring of the tides. In mild to moderate conditions, pleasure boats can safely cross the bar at the cost of some extra lumps (thrust up by the impact of sea swell upon shallows). The northerly segment of the bar hits less than twenty-three feet deep in places, and waves break readily here whenever the weather becomes the least bit severe.

The modern, sensual sailor is accustomed to the occasional foot-dampening rivulet of water running down the deck, but how many of us have stood in a fast-moving river of potatoes? Coastal schooners laden with spuds from Bodega Bay lost many an escaping deck load here in the old days, and they cursingly called this place the Potatopatch Shoal. Or so the favorite story goes. Many a yachtie since has had his own inner potatoes whipped and mashed in the Potatopatch on a bad night. This can be a discomfiting neighborhood even in moderate weather; in a blow, it should be avoided at all costs.

Northbound, anything smaller than a ship (definition: ships carry boats) will likely use the Bonita Channel, a narrow way leading between the Marin headland and the Potatopatch. Three red-flashing buoys mark its western border. A green-flashing, black buoy marks the shallow Sears Rock and Centissima Reef to landward; the channel's width in

Gremlins and Black Holes on the Southern Bar

This correspondent once blundered into just such a night on the southern bar and never even saw—but felt in the pit of the stomach—one wave that dropped straight away; the agonizing sensation of falling into a black hole ended in a solid "whack" at the trough. Marooned for an instant in a deep hole in the ocean, the helm of our thirty-foot yacht afforded an arresting perspective on the moving breaker that towered above briefly, then crashed down hard and cold. Hard enough, and spilling water deep enough, to touch a moment's wonder: Have we been cashed in?

Then our little champ popped up and out. I may have been needful of an easy breath on the top of that wave, but I could not help noticing the view. Up ahead, caught in the loom of the city, something more vast than a breadbox was breaking from all the way left to all the way right. And just when I had seen enough to *believe*, the bottom fell out again. It was three o'clock in the morning. Since the witching hour—after steering some nine hours—I had been seeing green gremlins dancing on the wavetops; now I was suffering visions of icy, dark fluids wriggling about my knees. Some wave. And on top of the second one was the same view. Grandaddy was *still* breaking. A little green gremlin perched atop the sheet winch saluted smartly and said, "Standing by to alter course, Sir!"

It was a tricky turn to avoid the danger of being caught broadside in the dark and being rolled all the way over. Thanks to a good hand on the sheets, we got away with it. That gremlin can sail with me anytime. In rosy recollection, that night has become one of the great thrills of my life. But I have not returned for a second ride. In a southerly, the forces on the bar come from more than one direction: two, perhaps three, wave patterns mix unpredictably, and the water develops a scent of treachery undesirable in the medium that supports one's vessel. Not on the suggested tour.

this portion is a mere three-tenths mile. Currents in the Bonita Channel run north to south through most of the tide cycle, the channel being protected from the ebb by Point Bonita, the "corner" at the tip of the strait's north shore. Currents ebb south to north for the two hours leading up to maximum ebb. In the rest of the cycle, water runs toward the south, first as an eddy to the ebb, later as flood that wraps around Point Bonita into the strait.

No colorful names are attached to the shoal south of the Gate, which shallows to as little as thirty-two feet. South Channel runs close to Ocean Beach, marked by two red-flashing bell buoys. This is not a deep channel, and it makes a poor choice for a foul day. The southern bar as a whole turns wicked in a blow, especially when a storm sets waves from the southwest across the prevailing northwest swell.

The Main Ship Channel runs out the Gate in an almost straight course, bearing slightly to starboard outbound. Where the channel cuts through the bar, the lane is two thousand feet wide and marked by eight buoys: four in line on the north side flashing white, and four in line on the south side flashing red. This keeps with the old rule, "Red right returning." An inbound vessel in the channel will have the red buoys on its right, the starboard side.

Depths in the channel are fifty feet or greater, maintained by dredging when necessary. Deep water runs between the buoys and the bar for about one-tenth mile to the south. To the north, there is deep water for a strip one-half mile wide except near Buoy 5, where a spur raises depths to thirty-five feet just outside the channel. Inbound ships keep to the south side, outbound ships keep to the north, and little boats keep out of the way.

Outside the bar's semicircular arm, depths average fifty feet. Then the sand bottom drops away steadily until it reaches a depth of one hundred feet at the "Lightship," a name San Francisco sailors will not let go, even though there has been no ship on that station since 1971. In the seventy-three years preceding, several ships came and went in the name of lightship service. The first went into duty in 1898. The last arrived in 1950, a 133-footer colored bright crimson with a working crew of sixteen, riding to an anchor rode a thousand feet long. Easy to spot but expensive to maintain, it was replaced in 1971 with the less personable but more efficient LNB, large navigational buoy.

Not only from nostalgia do sailors cling to calling it a lightship. The proper name is the unwieldy San Francisco Approach Lighted Horn Buoy SF. The pros at Vessel Traffic Service call it "the LNB." Positioned eleven miles from the Golden Gate Bridge, the red buoy is forty-two feet tall, forty feet in diameter, and weighs 104 tons. On a clear night, the flashing bright strobe is visible from the hills surrounding the Bay. The buoy carries enough fuel to power strobe, horn, and radio beacon for two years at a time. The generators hum day and night.

One mile east of the LNB is the pilot-boat cruising area, where San Francisco Bar Pilots board inbound vessels and disembark from outbound vessels. At all shipping ports of the West Coast, any foreign vessel and any American ship under register in the foreign trade is required to carry a pilot entering and leaving. If their masters are licensed pilots for these waters, American boats traveling coastwise may do without. San Francisco is the only port on the coast where pilot boats cruise on station continually. At Seattle or Long Beach or San Diego, pilots are available by appointment only.

In clear weather, navigation is easy in the Gulf of the Farallones, thanks to the prominence of landmarks ashore, and lights at Point Bonita, the LNB, Point Reyes, and the Farallones. In low visibility, those with the equipment will employ radar, LORAN, or satellite navigation. More commonly, however, they will use radio direction-finders, which show the bearing to radio beacons at Point Bonita, the LNB, Point Reyes, and the Farallones. No good sailor will go out lacking some method of homing in bad weather.

West of the LNB, the sandy bottom is mixed with patches

of mud and sand shells and deepens gradually to about 180 feet near the Farallon Islands. The main ship route westbound lies just south of the Farallones, a small, craggy rock colony interrupting some seven miles of ocean and marking the last vestige of the North American continent. Beyond the Farallones, the continental shelf drops precipitously, soon reaching depths greater than a mile.

The rocks and shoals of the Farallones present very real shipping hazards, especially for boats approaching from the north. The northern extremity, Fanny Shoal, is marked by a lighted buoy with whistle—a nice touch that surely would have been appreciated by the master of the clipper *Noonday*, who gave her name to the shallowest part of Fanny Shoal, Noonday Rock. Since 1862 the bones of the *Noonday* have mouldered, scattered on the bottom around a promontory reaching within thirteen feet of the surface.

For most sailors, the granite face of the Southeast Farallon is everything we need to know about the Farallones and everything we want to know. It is the closest to the Golden Gate, the largest, and—at an elevation of 350 feet—the most visible. Except for fishing boats on the hunt, it is the target for almost every excursion to the Farallones. Actually it is two islands, but the gap between is impassable. Seas build to massive proportions here, even on a mild day, as deep ocean swells uplift from the continental rise. Once a popular haunt for hunters and trappers, the Southeast Farallon now supports only a wildlife station and an automatized lighthouse; visitors are not allowed ashore. The portage is a dangerous one for the wildlife experts or for the Coast Guard, which services Farallon Light. The ocean surge wraps around the island, keeping the holding ground in an uncomfortable state almost always.

Sir Francis Drake stopped here for seal meat and eggs before leaving the region. The Russian–American Fur Company, which established a base on the Southeast Farallon much later, took a devastating toll—some 200,000 seals in three years. Under early American rule, the greatest damage was to the bird population: eggers from San Francisco took four million eggs a year. In boomtowns, these eggs fetched a dollar a dozen. Rival egg-picking companies battled each other in their own version of a range war until the government stepped in to halt the shooting. Fearing disruption to business, the eggers also resisted lighthouse builders, until in 1855 an armed expedition landed materials and workers for the construction of a light.

Egging was banned in 1897, and the islands became a wildlife refuge in 1909. By then the popular egg-laying murre had been reduced from four hundred thousand to less than ten thousand, but populations have been rebuilding since. The Farallones are the largest rookery in the country, with a dozen species living and breeding on the island and more than three hundred other varieties stopping in from their flyways.

In 1981 the islands became part of the Point Reyes–Farallon Islands National Marine Sanctuary, which takes in one thousand miles of Gulf waters, source of 40 percent of the Bay Area's crab catch, and birthing ground to elephant and harbor seals and sea lions. These waters are also home to blue and humpback whales, and they are a thoroughfare for the annual migration of gray whales from Arctic waters to spawning grounds in Mexico.

As islands go, the Farallones are not much, but in Northern California, they are what we have. Desolate Southeast Farallon is a memorable sight. Distant shoals toss spray high into the sunlight. Many have gone just to have a look, but there is no staying; and as a sublimation of tropical cruising dreams, a voyage up the Petaluma River is richer in rewards. The Southeast Farallon is often used as a turning mark for races, however, offering navigators the queasy prospect of determining just how tight is too tight a rounding in heavy swells, and how wide is too wide, given the race. In a typical northwest wind, a yacht leaving the Golden Gate can fetch or nearly fetch the island on starboard tack. Nearing the island, the crew will find them-

Then surveying the field General Grant declared, "I propose to fight it out on this line if it takes all summer!"

*This reaching strut will
thrust the spinnaker
afterguy, with its
dangerous loads, away
from the wire shrouds that
support the mast.*

selves leaving the Bay region's influence, both on currents and weather. As the sea turns to deeper blue and the swells build, winds will generally come more from the north, providing a starboard tack lift in the last few miles to the islands.

Currents Offshore

In the summertime, when the Pacific High Pressure Zone is active and generating northwesterly winds down the California coast, the predominant flow off the coast is a wind-driven current moving southeast at an average two-tenths knot: the California Current. Some five hundred miles wide, this flow closely duplicates Pacific weather patterns. Given ten to thirteen months, it will carry a raft to Hawaii. In the depths below the California Current is a compensating countercurrent headed north. During the winter, when the northwest wind is absent and winds blow often from southerly points of the compass, the California Current moves farther offshore. A northward-trending current builds inside it—a current that, in the latest thinking of oceanographers, represents the surfacing of the water that previously flowed six hundred feet below the California Current. Along the Northern California coast this northerly set, the Davidson Current, is active usually from November through February.

The California Current and the Davidson Current flow through ocean waters. In the shallower waters inside the Gulf of the Farallones, the currents are more variable, with strong influences from tidal flow through the Golden Gate. Just outside the San Francisco Bar is a slight current to the north and west, averaging one-tenth knot. Strong ebb tides can increase this Coast Eddy Current markedly, especially in periods of high river runoff, when current speeds may reach three knots. In such conditions, a muddy ebb-tide plume will spread nearly to the Farallones. In average conditions at the Lightship, tide-related currents reach three-tenths knot on the flood and four-tenths knot on the ebb, changing direction about 15 degrees each hour and covering the entire compass. The flow is described in a knotty diagram in NOAA's *Tidal Current Tables: Pacific Coast of North America and Asia.*

Tidal effects are the strongest forces in currents near the Golden Gate. The flood tide converges toward the strait, developing sooner along the shoreline north and south than near the Lightship. In the ebb cycle, most of the ebbing current flows straight out the Gate on a west–southwest heading through the Main Ship Channel—the line of least resistance. In the strait, Bonita Cove on the north and Baker Beach on the south are the sites of major eddies during both the flood and ebb tide cycles. Boats bound against the current—whether yachts or fishing vessels—will often duck into these backwaters rather than stem the flow in the middle of the channel. Flood currents tend to set straight in, with a slight northward tendency. Ebbs near Fort Point set slightly toward the south, a navigational hazard in low visibility.

Soggy Socks and Instant Oatmeal

Like the Bay itself, the waters beyond the Golden Gate are at their friendliest in the fall of the year. Temperatures tend to be mild then, with an easy sailing breeze and a light swell. This is likewise the time when most offshore cruisers pass through San Francisco, probably headed south from Seattle or Vancouver for an easy winter in Mexico. Voyages north from San Francisco hit a lucky streak from time to time, but usually the trip is a rough one, made against the prevailing wind and sea and against the harsh stuff common off the coast of the Pacific Northwest. Those same elements work in favor of the cruiser headed south, of course, and they prevail all the way to Cabo San Lucas at the tip of the Baja peninsula.

World cruiser Eric Hiscock was heard to comment on a

505s reach toward the city front in a light winter northerly.

visit to California that anyone who could manage this coast could sail anywhere. Not that these are the world's most extreme conditions; Hiscock was rather referring to the long distances between ports of call, the fog that makes visual piloting difficult, and the elements that nearly always oppose northbound traffic. Cruising to Southern California has the character of a lark. Cruising back has the character of work, especially when it comes to rounding windy Point Conception, the last promontory on the outer coast before the coastline turns sharply eastward toward Santa Barbara and Los Angeles. With the hot, desertlike regions of the Los Angeles Basin to goad them on, northwesterlies often howl and snort at Conception, earning it the nickname "Cape Horn of the Pacific."

It is not only the distance south that makes for Southern California's warmer climate. The Los Angeles Basin lies in a sharp coastal indentation, sheltered from the north by mountains. Northwesterlies bend and dissipate into this region in a weather pattern known as the Catalina Eddy. As offshore travelers know, and as every crew learns in the Transpac—the race from Los Angeles to Honolulu—outside the Catalina Eddy lies the exposed area known to southern weather forecasters as the outer coastal waters. Winds at westernmost San Nicholas Island may blow forty knots while sails are slatting at Newport Beach.

This differential between inner and outer coastal waters in the southland makes for engaging tactical decisions aboard racing fleets bound downcoast from San Francisco—how soon to risk "going in." And the frequently bruising weather along the coast north of Point Conception accounts for another phenomenon peculiar to San Francisco: the relative popularity of small-boats for downcoast racing. While a number of races have been institutionalized over the years, those meant for forty- and fifty-footers have had a hard go recently finding enough participants to make the thing matter. The Midget Ocean Racing Association, meanwhile, with its fleet of boats thirty feet and under, sponsors a very popular coastal race each July. Races have run to Ensenada, Morro Bay, and, most often, to San Diego. More bang for the buck is the MORA motto, but why the popularity? MORA boats can make the return trip on trailers—via Interstate 5.

The queue for the jibe mark.

VI: THOSE COMPETITIVE JUICES

When the hurly-burly's done,
When the battle's lost and won . . .
—THE WEIRD SISTERS OF "MACBETH"

You still gotta go with the flow.
—SURFER JOE

*T*HE EARNEST FOLK-WISDOM of the sailing world has it that wherever any two are gathered together in whatever name, they will race. They may, of course, pretend not to: this game can be felinely surreptitious, with no more than a nonchalant tweak on the genoa sheet or the cunningham when no one seems to be looking. The hard-core cruising soul is not immune to this compulsion to compete—especially if, after a nonchalant tweak, there seems to be a chance of winning. The next stage is full concentration—one eye crooked—*not* to look at the other boat. From the same fiber, with much overlapping temperament, comes formalized racing: with cannon-shot starts, engraved cheese trays, and, for some, total engrossment. "I think it'll work," said the young man about to tie the matrimonial knot. "We've been going together for years, and she's never kept me from a race yet."

On the Bay, the competitive scale covers international fleets at special events, evening round-the-buoys sociables, and all that passes in between. The Folkboats, a "woodies" one-design class, started evening racing in the 1960s. Many clubs and classes have followed suit, with varying emphasis on the competitive. Like the midwinter regattas, evening races are not approached with quite the serious demeanor of the summer-season weekend; they offer beginners their best chance to test the waters in a relaxed atmosphere, probably with mild winds and—probably—with strong currents. Some sponsors, including the Sausalito Cruising, Encinal, and Oakland yacht clubs, do not even require that entries be members of a club.

Race committees on the Bay enjoy a peculiar luxury. During the summer they can nearly always count on wind. Yet luxury is not without its price, practically and philosophically. Bay sailors who go away to race may have trouble adapting to "the kind of stuff the rest of the world sails in." On a Bay dominated by tidal strategists, wind direction and wind force are taken for granted: there is so often a narrow tidal lane where a boat *must* go to win. A contrast, that, to how a Midwestern lake sailor's success depends on reading the weather pattern in the sky (to choose the favored side of the course) then moment-by-moment "bouncing" from puff to puff, catching the wind-shifts toward the mark (the *lifts*). The San Francisco Bay sailor is a different creature, given to ignoring most anything outside of current flow. Crossing a patch of bad stuff, the San Franciscan may choose to live with a huge wind-shift away from the mark (a *header*) in order to reach the good water. Indeed, a tack in bad water could bring an undesired fame if it led, say, a five-knot boat into a three-knot, wrong-way current.

When a day comes when the westerly is late—or perhaps when a high-pressure cell squats overhead, incubating a heated calm and bare oddments for wind—the race committee's job becomes philosophical. Any site chosen for a weather mark may lie to leeward in ten minutes. To wait for the westerly or not to wait, that is the question. If there seems a reasonable chance it will come, most committees will wait, "to provide the fairest race possible." But what means "fair"? Jim DeWitt, a past national men's sailing champion, likes the kind of coping race that eccentric, light winds invoke. DeWitt believes there are competitive values beyond the textbook race. "Sailing in junk," he calls it. "It's good for you. There's character in it. Maybe it's just because I grew up sailing on Lake Merritt, and I feel at home in such stuff; but when you get outside the Bay, there's a lot of it to contend with. It's a trial, and it's honest. It's less physical and more mental than twenty-five knots."

Not that race committees will ever quit preferring textbook conditions as long as nature will allow, as it does reliably in a reliably windy place. A race committee setting up a summertime race course in the vicinity of the East Bay's Berkeley Olympic Circle will want to know which direction equals dead-to-windward. The committee will then lay a starting line between two boats (or between one boat and a buoy) on a perpendicular to the bearing to the windward mark. On the Berkeley Circle, it is even possible to set the starting line and the marks, then wait for the westerly, with a very high success rate. "Normal" westerlies are likely to come in at 205 to 215 degrees magnetic (magnetic compass readings were 16 degrees, 27 minutes east of true compass readings in 1981, with an annual decrease of three minutes). As the sea breeze develops, the wind will increase, probably shifting west to a bearing 220–230 degrees magnetic. Day after day, it happens.

But all this contributes further to the popular image of San Francisco Bay as a place where tides speak with a many-forked and swift tongue, where the winds blow hard and that is all there is to it. And this image, swallowed whole, hurts many people's chances for racing success. Currents indeed dictate strategy on the grand scale, but there are bobbles, windwise, that may turn the key between the also-ran and the ran-away-and-hid, especially in small boats. Boats short-tacking the city front against a flood tide will encounter significant lifts and headers. Each such windshift must be weighed against the currents of the moment. Where tacking to catch a lift takes a boat across a tide line and into a strong adverse current it would otherwise not encounter, not going is a good choice. Where tacking to catch a lift exacts no great penalty—where the difference between the relief ten yards off the rocks and forty yards off is worth less than the difference afforded by the windshift—go. A ten-degree shift well played will often carry a boat right by another that ignores it.

Especially along the beaches west of the Marina breakwater, there are periods during the tide cycle when the zone of general protection is broad and the zone of maximum protection is narrow—too narrow to occupy very long. As the fleet files its way along the city front, boats behind are hopelessly gassed by the leaders of the parade. An entire fleet will queue along a narrow lane of slightly-less-adverse current, with each boat spoiling the wind behind, and spoiling it worse rank by rank. The leaders—those few who have a shot at clear air—are likely to be led, eventually, by the boat that achieves the right balance between tidal concerns and windshifts. These two strategic concerns tend to be compatible here anyhow, since on most days the lifts come "from the beach" to lift port tack. This condition favors the boats "inside" on port tack, or closer to the beach (and thus in more tidally-protected water). A close-in line may also

Yes Virginia, there is a spinnaker up there.

mean lighter winds—near Crissy Field, in particular—so the navigator cannot sail with blinders on. In a forty-footer, one might be lucky to catch two usable windshifts on a two-mile beat against the tides. In a twenty-footer the options increase: a twenty-footer can shave the beach closer and accelerate more quickly out of a tack. In a tiny Snipe, an International 14, or a Fireball dinghy, the game is wide open. Tacks are instantaneous. So is acceleration. Brains and boat-handling will carry the day.

The fast pace of Bay sailing requires a thorough understanding of right-of-way to get everyone home in one piece. That includes right-of-way under the racing rules of the United States Yacht Racing Union and right-of-way under the rules of the road, which govern racers' encounters with nonracing boats. In a situation such as short-tacking the city front, rules need to be not merely understood but internalized in the reflexes of skipper and crew. The racing rules are lengthy; they are dealt with in detail as published by the USYRU, as well as a number of other excellent explanatory books. Unfortunately, there are people who have not read the rules in any form; and while it might be too much to bar them from the field, it would seem appropriate that they be preceded by a horseman with a lighted lantern.

Ponder USYRU Rule 43, "Close-Hauled, Hailing for Room to Tack at Obstructions." A boat that is "pinned" by another close by, as they approach the shore, is given the right to request room to tack, but *only* if it is impossible for her to tack without hitting the other boat. In a westerly, starboard tack takes Bay sailors toward the beach, with right-of-way. Port tack takes them away. A boat on port tack, once it is far enough from the rocks to tack back, has no special privileges; port tack must give way to starboard tackers even when that means ducking below them or taking that unwanted tack back toward the rocks before the time is right, before the speed is up. Multitiered overlaps and reasonable warning time come into the finer points of searoom at obstructions. But all of this must be dealt with

on the instant, in the midst of distractions. The real competitor will time tacks diabolically, to the worst advantage of opponents and the best advantage of self. This is how the game is played: sailshape, hullform, water, wind, and chess. And noise:

"STARBOARD! Searoom! STARBOARD! Searoom! Searoom!"

These cries ring loud on the city front, and the bigger the boat, the more allowance must be made as boats cross. Experts play it close when they are serious, but it is not uncommon in a tightly-bunched fleet for starboard-tack skippers to give ground to port tackers in the interest of mutual survival, shrugging off the foul involved in the knowledge they themselves will be in a port tack yacht momentarily, and it will be hard in crowded waters not to foul.

Cityfront, flood-tide beats—as well as mark roundings anywhere, anytime—are rich in protest-provoking encounters. But those who carry their beefs to protest must keep one matter in mind: their protests will very often be heard by well-meaning people who did not witness the incident and who, after an earnest search of the facts as found and after duly considering the nearly-inevitable conflicts in testimony, will rule according to the burden of proof. USYRU rules specify which boat must prove its case in right-of-way disputes. Where any doubt remains, that boat will be disqualified.

Odds and Odd Ends

Those who are successful at racing on the Bay measure each situation at the moment, then remeasure at the next. Races are not won by any rule of thumb that can be scribbled on the sleeve of a parka. And yet there are pointers that count for something, granted the skepticism they deserve.

Whether or not to "play the cone of Alcatraz" is a question that comes up, sometime during the season, for most cruiser-racers. The question is an endemic concern to Big Boat Series contestants in any flood-tide start. Run each September, the Big Boat Series (St. Francis Yacht Club's Perpetual Trophy Regatta) is the unofficial annual convention of West Coast yacht racing. It brings the cream of the international ocean-racing crop to four races around the buoys of the Bay.

Starts are made east of Alcatraz, near Treasure Island, with the first leg beating west from there to a special mark near Crissy Field. During an ebb tide—or very early in the flood, when a slight ebb current remains in the middle of the Bay and flood streams have developed along the shore—the choice westbound is obvious: keep to the middle, where the currents will help. As the ebb turns to flood, a flood-protected zone develops east of Alcatraz—the Alcatraz Cone—but its value varies at different hours. Early in the flood, a boat that beats to the island and plays it close will make better time than one that sails from the starting line direct to the city front, arriving at the Embarcadero and short-tacking from there. Up until maximum flood, in fact, there is an advantage in tacking "up the face" of Alcatraz, close along the San Francisco side of the island and into the "bubble" in the current that forms on the up-current (west) side. Many is the yacht that has profited from an extra couple hundred yards of relief while competitors bite the bullet, tacking off too early across the current to reach the city front. Boats as small as Stars (twenty-three feet) have used this ploy. Boats as large as *Windward Passage* (seventy-three feet) have also tasted the payoff.

Sooner or later, however, the advantage of the cone diminishes, even though the protected zone does not disappear. At about maximum flood, the best prerace plan (allowing for tactical shifts during the race) calls for beating westward into the cone behind Alcatraz, then crossing from the backside of the island to the city. At one hour after maximum flood, it usually pays to go straight to the city from from a Treasure Island start.

The neighborhood between Alcatraz and Angel Island sees heavy racing traffic, particularly when courses start and finish off the western face of Angel Island, Point Knox. The channel runs deep and currents run strong between Alcatraz and Angel, with Angel's shoreline affording some relief. In the photograph of flood-tide flow accompanying the discussion of tides and currents (chapter 3) a current split can be seen east of a line between Alcatraz and Angel. The current divides, some of it flowing onto the Berkeley flats, most of it turning into the channels, north or south. A westerly wind exhibits the same tendency, and a bend in the wind can be expected in this area. It will be less marked than the action of the currents: unconfined to the channels of the Bay, the winds carry on to the hills of Richmond, Albany, and Berkeley.

Go right. Go right. Without so much as stopping to consider, we have seen, already, exceptions to the "go right" rule. Yet it is a starting point for much tactical thinking about upwind legs on the West Coast. In Southern California, where currents are often tactically negligible, the reasoning involves developments, or likely developments, in the sea breeze. Coastal westerlies tend to increase through the day; and as they increase, they tend to bend, coming more from the north. By sailing toward the right side of the course—the northerly side—after the start, one is therefore sailing toward the increase, and sailing toward a port-tack header that equals a profitable, progressive starboard-tack lift toward the mark. The "go right" rule applies at all times—except, of course, when it pays to go left.

Starting lines at Point Knox, on Angel Island, invoke the go-right rule for tidal reasons. In a flood tide, a boat leaving Knox Buoy for a weather mark at Yellow Bluff will reach relief sooner by going right—toward Sausalito—and will expose itself to less direct flood current. When the tide turns to ebb, such a jog to the right leads into an ebb stream running from Raccoon Strait right toward the mark; a jog left will reach a powerful ebb stream in the Alcatraz Channel, but the last stretch then is likely to lead *against* the ebb from Raccoon Strait.

Yellow Bluff is a teaser to approach. Close under the bluff, the sailing is fraught with puffs from odd directions and holes in the wind induced by the hills of the headlands. In anything less than a stiff breeze, boats approaching the bluff will find the wind twisting, allotting advantages here and there that cannot be perfectly foretold. On average, any lifts on the way to the bluff will come from the breeze that flows through the Golden Gate, then puffs north into the relative vacuum caused by the bluff (in winds light to medium). Such occasions favor the inside on port tack, though the wind effect must be weighed against imperatives of the current.

The Berkeley Olympic Circle is a circular arrangement of buoys in the shallows of the East Bay. Two miles in diameter and lying entirely outside the channels—thereby protected from the fastest flow of the current—the Circle is a prime location for major championships and for any regatta that can squeeze in. With one sphere marking the center of the circle, a starting line can be laid at the center with the entire surrounding ring of buoys available for use as marks; for world championships, the entire buoy system may be replaced temporarily by special marks according to the wind of the moment.

The north end of the circle is too shallow for a six-foot draft, sometimes for less, but smaller boats fare well here despite the thrashing they take when a strong westerly sets slop over chop in the shallows. Ebb tides are notoriously lumpish on the circle; but in a breeze even a flood-tide condition can be rough, with the flood setting onto the flats and swirling north, almost cutting off the flow coming out of the Richmond Channel and persisting well after ebb currents begin—across the way—along the Tiburon shore.

A combination of wind and tidal factors mostly favors the right side of the course on the Berkeley Circle, (in a westerly, anyway) but not without qualification. While the right side tends to be favored, the far right corner may not be. Lifts and headers and—most of all—the need to sail in clear air, unaffected by other boats, will often argue against exploring the right corner. Tides involve strategy. Fleets involve tactics. There are great similarities from one day to the next in the strategic demands of the Circle, but no two tactical races are the same.

Oak, Ash, and Carbon Fiber

When Hemingway chose to tantalize his readers with a description of Lady Brett Ashley, he said she was "built with curves like the hull of a racing yacht." The mind filled in the rest. *The Sun Also Rises* was written in the twenties, when boats were built with curves like Brett Ashley's. The shallow, beamy, fin-keeled profile of a modern racing yacht, by way of comparison, might come closer to an insult. Black anodized winches, toggled hydraulics panels, and noodle-thin spars do not spell the romance of mahogany and brass. But they make deucedly effective machines.

Racing on the Bay runs a broad gamut. The springtime Master Mariners Regatta, a revival of the work-boat races of the 1800s, now brings out in force the classic yachts. The Birds, originated in the 1920s as "syndicate" boats for match racing, have since competed in thirteen matches for the San Francisco Perpetual Challenge Trophy; in the process, they have grown into an active class of twenty-three surviving boats (out of twenty-six built). Birds can be found on the starting line most any Sunday. No less classic is the El Toro, an eight-foot pram often built in wood to a design from the 1930s. The El Toro's annual Bullship Regatta, a Bay crossing from Sausalito to San Francisco, finishes at the St. Francis Yacht Club's line, right where races finish each

"She was built with curves like the hull of a racing yacht. . . ."

fall in the Big Boat Series—which is racing at its space-age best.

Organized racing on San Francisco Bay goes back to 1869, when, as an early order of business, the San Francisco Yacht Club staged the club's first regatta. The winner was the sloop *Emerald*, a dark-hulled lady with a graceful sheer and a cutter-styled bow. The newly-formed club started its race from the station of the time—at Mission Rock, just south of China Basin—reached south to a stakeboat at Hunters Point, and from there sped across the South Bay to a stakeboat near Oakland. Then came a beat west to a stakeboat near the Golden Gate and back to the start, rounding all marks.

Such a course is well-nigh unthinkable today, but those were simpler times. In place of the book-length "handicapping" rules applied to modern boats in the determination of time allowance, the San Francisco Yacht Club's sailing regulations by 1877 had developed so far as to recognize two classifications: schooners and sloops (with yawls lumped in with the schooners). In place of the complex time allowance tables of today's U.S. Yacht Racing Union, the club gave allowances of three-fourths minute per foot of waterline length; this allowance was changed in the 1880s to one minute per foot. Somebody always griped about being rated unfairly. Some things do not change.

An unusually large proportion of San Francisco Bay skippers sailed their own boats in those early days, more so than in the East. The famous yachts of the nineteenth century—the likes of the *Chispa*, *Casco*, or *Lurline*—were big things by present thinking. But not just the fat cats wanted to race: little boats came on the scene, from sailing canoes on up, and soon "Mosquito Regattas" sprang up to accommodate them. So successful was small-boat sailing that skippers decided they needed a forum of their own—which had a lot to do with getting the Corinthian Yacht Club started. And just to make sure it stayed a small-boat club, Corinthian Yacht Club's bylaws stated flatly that no boat over forty-five

feet would be admitted. Our perception of relative size has changed since then.

Our oldest major local prize is the San Francisco Perpetual Challenge Trophy, a big bite of silver first contested in 1895 under the auspices of the two senior clubs, San Francisco and Corinthian. In that first contest, the honors went to Encinal Yacht Club, whose *El Sueno* defeated San Francisco's *Queen*. The trophy has had a lively existence. Most matches are run between local clubs, but challenges come also from outside. The San Francisco Perpetual Challenge Trophy has spent some twelve years of its life at the Los Angeles and San Diego yacht clubs, causing no end of bother. Whenever a Southern California boat skips off with this one, minds are bent in earnest on getting it back.

In recent times, San Francisco Bay has acquired the starting line of not just one but two races to Hawaii. These are Ballena Bay Yacht Club's race to Kauai and the Singlehanded Sailing Society's solo race, also to Kauai. But the City By The Bay missed out on hosting the classic Transpac by a fault of its own—the San Andreas. In the dawning years of this century, Mr. Clarence MacFarland of Honolulu got it in his head that a race across the Pacific from California would be good for the sport of sailboat racing and good for the economy of the islands. To that end, he came yachting over in 1906 in his schooner *La Paloma*, expecting to stir up a race home from the lusty descendants of the Forty-Niners. Instead he found a tent city still smouldering, still in shock, and more in need of shelter and commerce than of a 2,500-mile lark. *La Paloma* sailed on to Los Angeles, where MacFarland found his race (and finished last). Transpacs still leave from Point Fermin, at the mouth of Los Angeles Harbor. But if the '06 quake and fire shook up sailing, the pieces quickly fell back together, albeit with new arrangements.

One of the problems confronting the crew of the Stone Boat Yard after the quake was how to hoist the sloop *Yankee* back into the cradle so they could finish her construction.

Stone's at that time was located about where the St. Francis Yacht Club stands today on the Marina seawall, which at the time was marshland. Ribbed and timbered fifty-two-foot yachts do not pick up handily once they have been dropped on the floor, but the Stone crew managed, and the *Yankee* grew to be a happy boat. In her first season, in 1907, she won the first ocean race out of San Francisco Bay.

Perhaps that race grew from a seed planted by Clarence MacFarland, perhaps it was simply time for it to happen. The course began in the strait, led around the Middle Farallon, and then home—more than sixty miles, figuring in tacking angles. San Francisco Yacht Club Commodore Francis Phillips put up the cup that *Yankee* won. The club still hosts this annual race, though with certain changes: the turning mark has been changed to the well-lighted, beaconed, nearer Southeast Farallon; the race has become part of the Danforth Ocean Racing Series, and it is only one of many races now that turn at the Farallones.

The *Yankee* has long since been rerigged as a schooner. She has not won an ocean race in quite a while, but she sails on, cutting a wake in the Master Mariners events and resting in her quiet hours in a cityfront berth close by her birthplace. Her beefy, varnished bowsprit aims right at the Marina Green. The volley balls *bomp* in the afternoon air.

The idea of sending men to sea to race, night and day of all things, and supposedly for pleasure, precipitated no end of tongue-clucking in 1907. It still has not ceased. By way of complete transformation, however, the popularity enjoyed by ocean racing today merits certain caveats. When invited along on an ocean race, and especially a long one, it is wise to pay careful attention to one's proposed companions. Before making a committment, apply the Oreo test. The trained eye can tell a lot about folks by the way they eat their Oreos. If none are provided by Providence, supply this vital research tool yourself. It is well worth the investment. Weigh closely the evidence. Does your watch captain wrench-and-split? If so, one-handedly or two? With the cookie in two halves, does this person scrape the icing off with the teeth? Using the upper or the lower teeth? Does this person instead lick the icing slowly, appreciatively gazing at the icing between licks? Or is a proposed watchmate the precise aesthete who will deftly wrench-and-split, maintaining all the icing in a smooth layer on one surface, inverting then the opposite half of the sandwich to imprint OᴚƎO before carrying the icing away? Or do we unveil in this test the souls of primitives who paw up cookies whole?

Choose well your long distance companions. No one who has been to sea soon forgets how big is the ocean, or how small is a boat.

Associations, Associations, Associations

Work expands to fill the space allotted. Associations expand to fill the universe. In 1928 came the first of many associations devoted to competition on San Francisco Bay: the Yacht Racing Association was formed and allied with the North American Yacht Racing Union (now, minus Canada, the U.S. Yacht Racing Union). Today the YRA umbrella subsumes many time-allowance and one-design classes, including those that race on the ocean. The YRA has a listing in the San Francisco telephone directory and is a good source of information for those wanting to get into the game.

Most YRA races around the Bay run long circuits, turning around any of a number of marks and finishing back where they started, under the eye of the race committee of the sponsoring club. Each spring, however, the YRA opens its season with a pair of races different from anything seen later—so different that the Coyote Point and Vallejo races are not counted toward points accumulated for the season championships. With half a thousand boats entered, the fleet is split into two groups, one fleet starting from the city front for Coyote Point Yacht Club on the peninsula and one fleet starting from Richmond for Vallejo Yacht Club at the

A foredeck hand aboard the 43-foot Wings
*clips the spinnaker's turtle bag to the
lifelines in anticipation of a tack, mark
rounding, and spinnaker set.*

mouth of the Napa River. These are routes not normally raced, and the Bull Run aspect justifies leaving them out of the season tallies: the fleets rest overnight at their respective destinations and race home the following day. There are no great tricks of the tide on either course, but the Vallejo trek can become quite variable in the way of wind, and such variability acts capriciously in its odds. Similar things happen on the dance floor of the Vallejo Yacht Club's Saturday night celebration, with the usual chastening effect Sunday morn, chastity unavailing.

The Small Boat Racing Association was formed in 1937 to handle the needs of three centerboard classes. The number of classes has grown to seventeen, but of the original three, only the Snipe remains. SBRA contests are held at many Bay locations, one of the favorites being the waters off Richmond. There, sheltered by Angel Island, lie some of the Bay's smoothest waters, contributing to the Richmond Yacht Club's reputation as a stronghold of small-boat sailing. A further advantage for these small boats lies in the options afforded a race committee in these waters to shift the race course north or south. In a westerly breeze, a move south—toward the Berkeley Circle—takes the race course more out of the lee of Angel Island and into the wind that funnels through the Golden Gate. If more wind is wanted, it is usually there for the taking. A move north takes the race course deeper into the island's lee for lighter winds. Besides the Bay, the SBRA circuit takes its one-design fleets inland to bask in weekends at Clear Lake, Lake Yosemite, or Stockton. SBRA events usually have a one-hour break between races. They once tried longer, but found retraining the crews too much trouble.

Many more organizations exist in the tradition of "if you don't like it, start your own." The Small Yacht Racing Association was formed in 1957 to cover the needs of small keelboats. There are the South Bay YRA, KIF (Knarr–IC–Folkboat), Youth Yacht Racing Association, and so on. Many, like the One-Design classes and Offshore Yacht Racing associations, are part of the YRA. As a network, this multitude forms a workable array that keeps the sport in gear. With familiarity, even the muddy acronyms begin to roll readily off the tongue.

Banana Splits

Certain maneuvers are basic to sailing. Personal lists vary, but none overlook the tack, the gybe, or the trimming and easing of sails to different points of the wind. Those on San Francisco Bay may add the broach. Certain boats are born to sail straight. Others are not. Many yachts designed in the last decade develop a hard mouth under spinnaker. They tend to be fat in the middle, pinched in the ends, and generously supplied with sail. And so we have those breezy Bay days with more spinouts than a Hollywood stock-car race, more banana splits than a Saturday at Schwabs.

Under spinnaker, a boat develops its power high above the deck. The spinnaker pulls forward and up, but the lines controlling it lead aft, to turning blocks near the transom. From the lower corners of the spinnaker—the *clews*—the afterguy leads through the end of the spinnaker pole and aft to the windward quarter. The sheet leads to the leeward quarter. The spinnaker's upward pull acts upon the stern, then, tending to drive the bow down. Should the sail begin to oscillate—and draw the boat with it—the effectiveness of the rudder is imperilled roll by roll. Those flat topside sections near the bow make a dandy skid surface should the boat trip. To prevent a trip (to keep the boat on its feet) takes deft coordination between trimmer and helmsman. If the boat is momentarily overpowered—if the helmsman is losing—a quick *big* ease of the spinnaker sheet may save the moment. Easing the sheet depowers the sail. If that is accomplished before all rudder control is lost, it is likely that control will not be lost, after all. As the rudder digs in, some on-the-instant retrimming will prevent a violent popping of the rig as the spinnaker (chute/kite/thirdsail) refills: *bang!* When the sailing gets tough, and before disaster strikes, "choking" the chute is worth a try: ease the spinnaker pole forward and down: this depowers the sail and improves the odds of tracking straight.

The rain falls on the just and unjust. Sooner or later, for richer or for poorer, you will go down. The trick is to go down but not out. Top ocean-racing crews take it for granted the spinnaker will stay up no matter how high the wind—until the best helmsman on the boat crashes more than once. To take that attitude, they have to be confident of their ability to handle a knockdown (broach/spinout/banana split). As Han Solo put it, "Don't ever tell me the odds."

Aside from keeping close to the deck and out of the way of anything that might break, all the things one should do while the boat is broached are things that will contribute to regaining rudder control. One of the things the helmsman can do is *not* saw away at the thing. In the frustration (and embarrassment?), it is tempting to allow oneself a few convulsions on the helm, but yanking at it is useless—or, worse—counterproductive. The rudder is stalled. If the rudder were not stalled, we wouldn't *be* in this position, right? The rudder is not working; it must be made to work.

If Warwick "Commodore" Tompkins were explaining his personal set of numbers on how to escape from a state of broached-flat extremity, we would be hearing the words of a man whose boat-handling credentials are second to none. The first thing he would tell us is, "Let the boat go. The boat wants to go, so let it go. Straighten the rudder." The very form of the hull, Tompkins would say, wants to squirt ahead. In spite of everything else that happens through the broach, the hull will keep way on, and it will not turn into the wind much further than the beam.

Left to take its head, a thirty-seven-footer will make a likely three or four knots through the water, and speed is the key. To be sure, it will be making speed in the wrong direction, and the sails will shake up a terrible, unnerving din. Ignore all that. Enjoy it. Take a ride on the adrenalin. The mast probably will not break. The sail probably will not rip and the day probably will not end. While riding it out, waiting for speed, it may help to trim the mainsail slightly for a little more drive (although never on a small boat). Where trimming the main is used as a recovery technique, the emphasis is on the *slightly*. The sail is not supposed to look pretty—yet. And whoever does the trimming must understand that when the boat recovers, the mainsheet must run, pronto.

As the boat gains speed, water will speed over the rudder. This flow makes the rudder effective, and at last something can be done. There will come a moment when the boat seems ready to yield. It is time then to set the bit and turn the beast to course, being careful as Hey–Ho–Up she rises, not to trip right into an overcorrection in the opposite direction—wrong twice.

Because the boat is beam-on the wind in a knockdown, the boat will also stand beam-to the waves, excepting special cases. The waves on the ocean are probably big enough to matter, even enough to govern the critical moment for making the turn. Choose the wrong moment and the wave will rudely shove you back to where you started or worse. Choose the right moment, catch the wave just so, and you are on your way back to the good life (there being few thrills to compare with a slippery boat making fast tracks downwind, with every string bow-tight, under almost-too-much sail). The Bay in ebb tide beneath a healthy westerly will kick up waves enough for the helmsman of a small- to medium-size boat to employ them in a knockdown. Striking the hull, the wave will perhaps press the boat to a greater angle of heel. Passing underneath, and going away, the same wave turns the boat more upright. This turn aims the rudder more toward the down position—the working position—which makes for a splendid moment to engage the helm.

While the helmsman is choosing his moment, certain useful enterprises are available to the crew. By the time a

Sailpower, wavepower, and the Olympic-class Star.

boat becomes fully knocked down, the spinnaker sheet should have already run (though some drivers, in some circumstances, will ask that the sheet not be eased). Crew-weight belongs on the high side and aft—the maximum leverage point for kicking the bow around to a civilized course. If the *vang*—or preventer strap—holds the main boom in the water, ease the vang. If, on the opposite broach, the vang holds the main boom up in the air, ease it. The mainsail should be eased fully unless the skipper requests trim. Somebody should stand ready to ease a trimmed mainsheet or to trim an eased preventer at the instant of recovery.

If the boat is broached "to leeward," that means the lee rail has hit the water in the spinout. If the boat is broached "to weather," that means the weather rail went down. The main boom then is sticking up in the air and the spinnaker pole is aimed right down at the water. It is important in a knockdown-to-weather not to ignore the foreguy. If the spinnaker pole is going to go into the water, the foreguy must be eased—and not merely eased: *cast off*. The spinnaker pole can then rise; it must never be allowed to dig in: once in the water, under way, the spinnaker pole develops tremendous loads and transfers them to the mast at a point where the mast is unsupported. The mast-breakage curve thus steepens sharply when the spinnaker pole gets wet.

Also among the blunders available to the hardworking crew is one that is worse than most, and among the easiest to make: releasing the afterguy instead of the sheet. Aboard boats that are raced hard, sails are retrimmed with such frequency the afterguy may not be cleated at the moment of the knockdown. As the driver starts piping a jittery "Ease the sheet, Flibber. *Ease* it!", the person holding the tail of the afterguy is going to experience a strong reflex to ease the thing in hand. As a basic mistake in one of the Bay's basic maneuvers, easing the afterguy invokes an entertaining array of consequences: the sail flies farther from the boat; it wants to fill no matter how much the sheet is eased; being so far from the boat, it creates very effective sideways drag; and, being so far from the boat, it will be very hard to control when, at last, the boat stands up. A good set of procedures for one caught holding the afterguy in a knockdown is: (1) cleat that sucker, and (2) repeat the silent mantra: "I am controlling the afterguy. It must not be eased. I am controlling the afterguy. I am."

Now isn't that just like San Francisco Bay? It will send you off talking to yourself, every time.

EPILOGUE

*H*ALFWAY BETWEEN PAIN AND PARADISE lives the sailor of San Francisco Bay. That is where we introduced him, and that is where we must leave him. Chilled flat, thrilled sideways, broached to the gills, repeating the mantra of the moment:

Don't saw away at the helm. Straighten the rudder.
Climb to the high side quickly, quickly.
DUMP the spinnaker sheet. Stand ready to retrim.
I mean for *years* we've been going together. It'll work out.
I am controlling the afterguy. It must not be eased.
Being of the limp, gimp, wimp, and simper school . . .

Fortunately, anyone who wants to can likely sail a lifetime on San Francisco Bay without ever landing, so, on the ear. By avoiding races, or even by avoiding heavy-air spinnaker races in skittish boats, life can be kept (almost) peaceful. The sailing will be as dignified as the pelicans' stately flight. And yet the pointers and the nonpointers, thrill-seekers and still-seekers sail on the same water, under the same sky, under ultimate benevolences and stringencies alike. Those who would join them must take this to heart. One hand for ship, one for self. *And when somebody says "Heads up!" good gosh. Put your head down.*

INDEX